The Art of

Spelling

Jenny Pearson

The Art of Spelling

Jenny Pearson

Kivett Publishing

ISBN: 978-1-941691-40-3

Language Arts > Spelling

TABLE OF CONTENTS

INTRODUCTION

Why is it challenging to spell words correctly?

- Similar letter patterns can make different sounds.

  tough / though / through / thought

- There are multiple ways to make the same sound.

  rain / play / they / make / eight / break

- Technical jargon sometimes adds confusion.

We avoided technical jargon to help make the concepts clear. (For those who wish to learn the technical terms, these are collected in the Appendix.)

- Students need practice that helps build confidence.

Use the key at the back of the book to check your work.

- It helps to feel comfortable with the resources.

We attempted to make this book appeal to all ages. Teens and adults may appreciate the lack of pictures, and some kids appreciate this, too.

TIPS

Remember to check your answers to the exercises with the answers tabulated at the back of this book.

Reading and writing help with visual memory. Write troublesome words down several times on a sheet of scratch paper. Read regularly as this aids in spelling recognition (and also helps to improve fluency with English grammar).

In the summer of 2018, this book will also become available as an audio book. This will help you listen to the proper pronunciation as you read the words. You should also practice saying the words yourself if you need help with phonics.

VOWEL SOUNDS

(A Brief Intro)

- the long **a** sound:

  make (a_e) / play (ay) / they (ey) / rain (ai)

  angel (a) / eight (ei) / break (ea) / ballet (et)

- the long **e** sound:

  see (ee) / team (ea) / key (ey) / these (e_e)

  brief (ie) / ceiling (ei) / happy (y) / me (e)

- the long **i** sound:

  ice (i_e) / night (igh) / pie (ie) / try (y) / mind (i)

- the long **o** sound:

  no (o) / boat (oa) / phone (o_e) / grow (ow)

  toe (oe) / though (ough) / ou (shoulder)

- the long **u** sound:

  new (ew) / moon (oo) / tune (u_e) / through (ou)

true (ue) / flu (u) / fruit (ui) / soup (ou) / do (o)

- the short **a** sound:

    cat (a) / laugh (au) / plaid (ai)

- the short **e** sound:

    bed (e) / ready (ea) / friend (ie) / said (ai)

    says (ay) / any (a) / leopard (eo) / bury (u)

- the short **i** sound:

    is (i) / gym (y) / build (ui)

    women (e) / women (o) / business (u)

- the short **o** sound:

    hot (o) / father (a)

- the short **u** sound:

    cup (u) / ton (o) / blood (oo)

    trouble (ou)

- the **aw** sound:

    saw (aw) / cause (au) / taught (augh)

long (o) / talk (al) / bought (ough)

- the (short) **oo** sound:

book (oo) / could (ou) / push (u) / wolf (o)

- the **y +** long **u** sound:

use (u_e) / few (ew) / view (iew)

value (ue) / coupon (ou) / beauty (eau)

- the **y + oo** sound:

cure (u_e) / furious (u_i) / fury (u_y)

- the **oi** sound:

oil (oi) / boy (y) / buoyant (uoy)

- the **ow** sound:

cow (ow) / out (ou) / drought (ough)

- the soft **uh** sound:

a (a) / the (e) / ago (a)

item (e) / cousin (i) / carrot (o) / circus (u)

vinyl (y) / nation (io) / bargain (ai) / famous (ou)

- the 'l sound, which involves a much reduced **uh** sound coming after a **t** or a **d** (but not after **nd**):

  title (le) / vital (al)

- the 'n sound, which involves a much reduced **uh** sound coming after a **t** or a **d** (but not after **st** where **t** is silent):

  kitten (en) / carton (on)

- the **ir** sound:

  her (er) / sir (ir) / word (or) / turn (ur)

  pearl (ear) / syrup (yr) / nourish (our)

- the **w +** short **u** sound:

  one (o)

- the **w +** long **i** sound:

  choir (oi)

- vowel **+ r** sounds:

short e **+ r**: care / chair / their / there / bear

short o **+ r**: car / farm / heart / sergeant

o **+ r**: more / for / four / war / door / roar

Note: You probably hear **more** and the other words above with the long **o** sound. (For technical reasons, they are classified as **aw + r**, but if you try to say **aw** when you say these words, it won't come out right.) Try to say long **o + r** when pronouncing the words above.

the ir sound: her / sir / word / turn / pearl

short i **+ r**: ear / near / here / cheer / pier

uh **+ r** : over / doctor / collar

long i **+ r**: fire

oo **+ r**: poor / tour

y **+ oo + r**: cure

ow **+ r**: sour

CONSONANT SOUNDS

(A Brief Intro)

- the **b** sound:

    big (b) / rabbit (bb)

- the **ch** sound:

    chin (ch) / watch (tch) / future (tu)

    question (ti) / righteous (te)

- the **d** sound:

    dog (d) / ladder (dd) / could (ld) / spelled (ed)

- the **f** sound:

    fun (f) / offer (ff) / phone (ph)

    rough (gh) / half (lf) / often (ft)

- the **g** sound:

    good (g) / egg (gg) / ghost (gh)

    guy (gu) / vague (gue)

- the **h** sound:

hat (h) / who (wh)

- the j sound:

  jet (j) / page (ge) / giant (gi) / gym (gy)

  edge (dg) / soldier (di) / gradual (du)

- the k sound:

  kid (k) / cat (c) / back (ck) / school (ch)

  soccer (cc) / talk (lk) / unique (qu) / box (x)

- the l sound:

  like (l) / tall (ll) / able (le)

  castle (tle) / island (sl)

- the m sound:

  mom (m) / summer (mm) / thumb (mb)

  calm (lm) / autumn (mn)

- the n sound:

  nap (n) / funny (nn) / knee (kn)

  gnat (gn) / pneumonia (pn)

- the **ng** sound (no clear **g** sound is heard, yet the **ng** sound is different from the **n** sound, as we will learn in Part 2):

  ring (ng) / tongue (ngue) / pink (nk)

Note: **pink** ends with the **ng + k** sounds.

- the **p** sound:

  pet (p) / happy (pp)

- the **r** sound:

  run (r) / carry (rr) / write (wr) / rhyme (rh)

- the **s** sound:

  sun (s) / toss (ss) / ice (c)

  scent (sc) / psychology (ps) / castle (st)

- the **sh** sound:

  shy (sh) / tension (si) / sure (su) / special (ci)

  ocean (ce) / chef (ch) / motion (ti)

- the **t** sound:

  toy (t) / little (tt) / hoped (ed)

- the **th** sounds (two different kinds):

  the (*th*) / thing (th)

- the **v** sound:

  vine (v) / gave (ve) / of (f)

- the **w** sound:

  win (w) / why (wh) / penguin (u) / one (o)

- the consonant **y** sound:

  yes (y) / unique (u) / onion (i)

- the **z** sound:

  zoo (z) / buzz (zz) / was (s)

  scissors (ss) / xylophone (x)

- the **zh** sound:

  usual (s) / azure (z) / television (si)

  equation (ti) / beige (ge) / luxury (x)

PART 1

SPELLING

VOWELS

THE SILENT E RULE

mak[e] / thes[e] / tim[e] / phon[e] / tun[e]

When the letter **e** appears at the end of a word, it is usually silent. The pattern vowel **+** consonant **+** silent **e** helps to make a long vowel sound. For example, compare the pairs of words below.

at (short a) / [ate] (long a, silent e)

rid (short i) / [ride] (long i, silent e)

not (short o) / [note] (long o, silent e)

us (short u) / [use] (long u, silent e)

The patterns vowel **+** consonant **+ ing** and vowel **+** consonant **+ y** similarly help to make a long vowel sound. See the examples below.

rat (short a) / [rat]ing (long a)

tin (short i) / t[iny] (long i)

Circle the word that best fills in the blank.

1. I feel _____. My leg barely even hurts.

fin / fine

2. You're a good _____. Thank you for helping out.

pal / pale

3. The ball rolled down to the bottom of the _____.

slop / slope

4. Place your gum inside a piece of folded _____ paper.

scrap / scrape

5. Did you see that _____ fly over the mountain?

airplan / airplane

6. Does that amount _____ tax?

includ / include

7. We are _____ for an invitation.

hopeng / hoping / hopong

8. It was _____ under the big tree.

shade / shadi / shady

THE LONG A SOUND

rain / play / they / make / eight

The long **a** sound is commonly spelled using the **a_e** rule, where a single consonant appears between the **a** and the **e**. In these words, **e** is silent.

a̲t̲e̲ / c̲ak̲e̲ / s̲am̲e̲ / m̲az̲e̲ / s̲af̲e̲

There are similar **a_i** and **a_y** rules, but in these cases the **i** or **y** isn't silent.

m̲ak̲ing / a̲g̲ing / gr̲ad̲ing / b̲ab̲y / cr̲az̲y

When the long **a** sound is followed by the **n+j** sounds, it is usually spelled **ange**.

angel / change / strange / danger / arrange

When the long **a** sound is followed by the **s+t** sounds, it is usually spelled **aste**.

taste / waste / paste / haste / tasty

When the long **a** sound is followed by the **b+l** sounds, it is usually spelled **able.**

able / table / stable

When the long **a** sound comes at the end of a word, it is usually spelled **ay.**

day / say / pay / stay / way

Note the plural noun and verb tense forms of the **ay** rule.

days / ways / plays / played / stays / stayed

Occasionally, the long **a** sound is spelled **ey** (instead of **ay**) at the end of a word. (Note that the color **gray** is sometimes spelled **grey.** Both are correct.)

they / grey / obey / survey / convey

Sometimes, the long **a** sound is spelled **ai** instead of using the **a_e** rule. Many of these words end with **d, l, n, t,** or **nt.**

aim / mail / brain / paid / trail / paint

Occasionally, the long **a** sound is spelled **ei.**

beige / vein / reins

When the long **a** sound is spelled **ei**, it may be in the form **eigh** (with a silent **gh**). This often happens before a **b** or **t** sound, but can also occur at the end of a word.

eight / neighbor / weigh / freight / weight

Rarely, the long **a** sound is spelled **ea.** It is worth memorizing the following common words.

break / steak / great

Rarely, the long **a** sound is spelled **et** at the end of a word with multiple syllables.

ballet / valet / filet / gourmet / ricochet

A few more rare cases of the long **a** sound include:

- **aigh** like **straight** (**ai** normally makes a long **a**)

- **a** like **bass** (the musical sound)

- **au** like **gauge** (**au** normally makes an **aw** sound)

Circle the word that best fills in the blank.

1. I _____ my knee when I was roller skating.

> **scraped / scraiped / screiped / scrayped**

2. This morning, breakfast was served on a _____.

> **tra / trai / tray / treigh**

3. The cats are _____ a mouse.

> **chasing / chaising / chaysing / cheasing**

4. We rode on a _____ during our vacation.

> **trane / train / trein / treighn**

5. I bought three pairs of shoes for _____ dollars.

> **aty / aity / eity / eighty**

6. Did you feel the ground _____ last night?

> **shak / shake / shaik / shayk**

7. He isn't a _____. He is my cousin.

> **stranger / strainger / straynger / streinger**

8. The dog never _____ far from home.

> **strade / straid / strayed / streighed**

THE LONG E SOUND

me / see / team / key / needy

The long **e** sound is commonly spelled **ea**.

each / seat / teach / beat / dream

The long **e** sound is sometimes spelled with a double **ee** (usually in the middle of a word).

bee / peek / seed / wheel / teeth

The long **e** sound is sometimes spelled **ie** (usually in the middle of a word). This often happens before an **f** or **v**. Note that the **ie** spelling rarely follows the letter **c**.

brief / field / niece / movie / believe

When the long **e** sound comes after the letter **c**, it is often spelled **ei**. If you memorize the phrase, "i before e, except after c," it can help you remember this rule.

ceiling / receipt / deceit / deceive / perceive

The long **e** sound is sometimes spelled using the **e_e** rule, where a single consonant appears between the two e's. In these words, the final **e** is silent. This usually occurs at the end of a word, often with two syllables.

th**e**s**e** / **e**v**e** / comp**e**t**e** / **e**v**e**ning / extr**e**m**e**

At the end of a word, the long **e** sound is often spelled with a single **y**.

happy / baby / daddy / party / hungry

Rarely, at the end of a word the long **e** sound is spelled **ey**.

key / valley / money / monkey / journey

Sometimes, the long **e** sound is spelled with a single **e**. This happens with many pronouns (like **me** or **she**), and is common with words that begin with a prefix like **be** or **pre** (but the prefix **re** often makes a short i sound).

me / he / she / we / be

become / between / preschool

A few more rare cases of the long **e** sound include:

- i like **ski**

- **eo** like **people**

- **oe** like **phoenix**

Note that a few ways of spelling the long **e** sound can also be used to spell the long **a** sound:

- **ea** usually makes a long **e** sound, like **teach** and **dream**, but occasionally makes a long **a** sound, like **break**, **steak**, and **great**.

- **ei** usually makes a long **a** sound, like **eight** and **beige**. However, **ei** instead makes a long **e** sound, like **ceiling** and **receipt**, when it follows a **c**.

- **ey** usually makes a long **a** sound, like **obey** and **survey**. However, **ey** instead makes a long **e** sound, like **valley** and **monkey**, when it follows **k**, **l**, or **n**.

Circle the word that best fills in the blank.

1. My favorite pair of _____ is two years old.

> **jeens / jeans / jiens / jeins**

2. We painted my room light _____.

> **green / grean / grien / grein**

3. My sister loves sports. She is a great _____.

> **athleet / athlete / athliet / athleit**

4. I was _____ to win the game last night.

> **luckee / lucky / luckey / lucki**

5. Would you like a _____ of my chocolate chip cookie?

> **peece / peace / piece / peice**

6. I _____ your package in the mail this morning.

> **receeved / receved / recieved / received**

7. My dog _____ to go outside while it was raining.

> **reefused / refused / riefused / reifused**

8. Do you think Santa Claus could fit down our _____?

> **chimnee / chimny / chimney / chimni**

THE LONG I SOUND

I / try / time / night / pie

The long i sound is commonly spelled using the i_e rule, where a single consonant appears between the i and the e. In these words, e is silent.

ice / bite / time / ride / write

There are similar i_i and i_y rules, but in these cases the i or y isn't silent. (Exceptions to these rules include city, live, and giving, which don't have a long i.) Note that the second i in timing and riding isn't long.

icy / timing / riding / shiny / bicycle

The long i sound is sometimes spelled ie. This often happens before a d or s. Note that the ie spelling rarely follows the letter c.

lie / cries / cried / tried / tries

At the end of a short word, the long i sound is often spelled with a single **y**.

cry / why / fly / try / sky

The long i sound is sometimes spelled **igh**. This often happens before a **t**.

high / fight / bright / sight / delight

Occasionally, the long i sound is spelled with a single i. For example, this happens in some words ending with **ind** or **ild** and a variety of multi-syllable words.

I / mind / kind / child / wild / climb

final / pilot / rival / pirate / virus

A few more rare cases of the long i sound include:

- **eigh** like **height** (**eigh** normally makes a long **a**)

- **ai** like **aisle** (**ai** normally makes a long **a**)

- **uy** like **buy** or **guy**

- **is** like **island**

Circle the word that best fills in the blank.

1. I really wanted to _____ it, but it was the truth.

   deni / deny / denigh / denie

2. We _____ go there, depending on the weather.

   mite / myte / might / miet / meit

3. The peaches are _____. They taste delicious.

   ripe / rype / righp / riep / reip

4. I felt _____ when the lights went out.

   blined / blyned / blind / bliend / bleind

5. My mother makes me keep my room clean and _____.

   tidy / tydy / tighdy / tiedy / teidy

6. My sister _____ to several colleges this year.

   applide / applyed / applied / appleid

7. The librarian asks everyone to be _____.

   silent / sylent / sighlent / sielent / seilent

8. It's too expensive. I can't afford to _____ it today.

   by / bigh / bie / buy / bye

EI AND IE

The letters **ei** and **ie** each make two different sounds:

- **ei** often makes the long **a** sound like **vein**. When **ei** follows **c**, it makes the long **e** sound like **ceiling**.

  ei (after **c**) **ceiling / receipt / deceive**

- **ie** often makes the long **e** sound like **brief**. When **ie** comes near the end of a verb, it often makes the long **i** sound like **cries**. In plurals, **ie** usually makes the long **e** sound like **cities**.

  ie (not after **c**) **brief / field / tried / flies**

The rule "**i** before **e** except after **c**" can be helpful, but it has some exceptions. The most notable exception involves **ei** words that make the long **a** sound, like **vein** and **weight**.

  ei (long **a** sound) **eight / beige / neighbor**

Some exceptions to the "**i** before **e** except after **c**" rule:

- When **ei** makes a long **a** sound, like **eight** and **vein**, **e** comes before **i** even when they don't follow **c**.

- Other examples where **e** comes before **i** even when they don't follow **c** include **either, neither, weird, height, seize, being, seeing, leisure, forfeit, foreign**, and **counterfeit**.

- After a **c**, when **ie** doesn't make the long **e** sound, **i** often comes before **e** even when they do follow **c** like **ancient, science, society, fanciest**, and **sufficient**.

- One common example where **i** comes before **e** even when they do follow **c** and where **ie** makes the long **e** sound is the word **species**.

Circle the word that best fills in the blank.

1. The helium balloon flew up to the _____ .

ceiling / cieling

2. Our classroom is getting low on school _____ .

suppleis / supplies

3. That optical illusion is really _____ .

deceiving / decieving

4. It's my _____ that hard work will pay off.

beleif / belief

5. We sat down at the end of the _____ and fished.

peir / pier

6. My friend just moved to my _____ .

neighborhood / nieghborhood

7. Our dad takes a _____ approach to cooking.

scientific / sceintific

8. You don't want to eat snails. Well _____ do I!

neither / niether

-Y ENDINGS

The letter **y** can make two different sounds at the end of a word:

- **y** usually sounds like a long **e** at the end of a word with two or more syllables, like **happy** and **baby.**

  funny / mommy / daddy / city / shady

- **y** usually sounds like a long **i** at the end of a word with one syllable, like **sky** or **try.**

  by / cry / why / dry / sly

There are a few exceptions to these rules:

- A few words have two syllables, yet the **y** still makes the long **i** sound, like **deny** and **retry.**

- If there is a vowel before the **y**, like **ey** or **ay**, it may break these rules, like **key, they,** or **say.**

THE LONG O SOUND

no / boat / phone / grow / toe

The long **o** sound is sometimes spelled **oa**.

road / coat / soap / goat / toast

The long **o** sound is sometimes spelled using the **o_e** rule, where a single consonant appears between the **o** and the **e**. In these words, **e** is silent.

r|os|e / n|ot|e / p|ok|e / z|on|e / st|on|e

There are similar **o_i** and **o_y** rules, but in these cases the **i** or **y** isn't silent. (Exceptions to these rules include **done**, **moving**, and **agony**, which don't have a long **o**.)

j|ok|ing / p|on|y / h|op|ing / sm|ok|y / qu|ot|ing

The long **o** sound is sometimes spelled **ow**. This often happens at the end of a word.

own / show / elbow / window / tomorrow

The long **o** sound is sometimes spelled with a single **o** at the end of a syllable. This often happens when a word has multiple syllables.

go / total / ago / oval / program

The long **o** sound sometimes takes part in the group **ol**, when another consonant like **t** or **d** follows the **ol**. (The **l** isn't silent here.)

gold / cold / fold / bolt / revolt

Some less common cases of the long **o** sound include:

- **ou** like **shoulder**

- **oe** like **toe**

- **oble** like **noble**

- **ough** like **though**

- **ew** like **sew**

- **ao** like **pharaoh**

- **both** and **gross** (long **o** before two consonants)

Circle the word that best fills in the blank.

1. Don't try to use that radio. It is _____.

broaken / broken / browken / broughken

2. May I please _____ a pencil to do my homework?

borroa / borrow / borro / borrough

3. We watched our paper boat _____ on the water.

float / flote / flowt / flot

4. I already poured cereal into your _____.

boal / bole / bowl / boll

5. I'm trying to _____ the camera on it.

foacus / fowcus / focus / foecus

6. My grandfather _____ me that story last summer.

toald / towld / told / tould

7. I don't feel well today. I have a sore _____.

throat / throte / throwt / throt

8. How did you hurt your _____?

shoalder / showlder / sholder / shoulder

THE LONG U SOUND

new / tune / moon / true / through / lose

The long **u** sound is sometimes spelled with a double **oo**.

noon / loop / spoon / choose / balloon

The long **u** sound is sometimes spelled using the **u_e** rule, where a single consonant appears between the **u** and the **e**. In these words, **e** is silent.

tube / flute / super / assume / parachute

There are similar **u_i** and **u_y** rules, but in these cases the **i** or **y** isn't silent.

ruby / tuning / duty / assuming / dutiful

The long **u** sound is sometimes spelled with a single **u** at the end of a syllable. This often happens when a word has multiple syllables.

flu / tuna / lunar / tuba / brutal

The long **u** sound is sometimes spelled with a single **o**.

This often occurs before **m, v, s,** or at the end of a word.

do / who / whom / move / lose / prove

The long **u** sound is sometimes spelled **ui**. This often

happens before an **s, c,** or **t**.

fruit / juice / suit / cruise / recruit

The long **u** sound may be spelled **ou** between consonants.

soup / group / cougar / through / acoustics

At the end of a word, the long **u** sound may be spelled **ew**.

new / stew / dew / shrewd / brew

At the end of a word, the long **u** sound may be spelled **ue**.

blue / clue / due / true / issue

A couple of unusual cases of the long **u** sound include:

- **oe** like **shoe**

- **eu** like **neutral**

Circle the word that best fills in the blank.

1. I _____ the answer to that question.

knoo / knew / knu / knue

2. Quit acting like a _____. It's driving me crazy.

loonatic / lewnatic / lunatic / lounatic

3. We watched _____ when we woke up in the morning.

cartoons / cartewns / cartunes / cartouns

4. I measured its length using a _____.

rooler / rewler / ruler / rouler

5. The golfer followed the same _____ for every shot.

rootine / rewtine / rutine / routine

6. This chicken is plump and _____.

joocy / jewcy / jucy / juicy

7. My mom bought me a new pair of _____ today.

shoos / shews / shuse / shoes

8. We _____ my cat from the tree.

rescooed / rescewed / rescude / rescued

THE Y + LONG U SOUND

use / cute / few / view / beauty

Sometimes, the long **u** sound begins with a consonant **y** sound (like the word **you**) even when there isn't a **y** in the word. Compare the words in the examples below.

new (n + long u) / few (f + y + long u)

flute (f + l + long u + t) / cute (c + y + long u + t)

shoes (sh + long u + z) / use (y + long u + z)

The consonant **y** + long **u** sound is sometimes spelled with a single **u** at the beginning of a word.

used / unique / usual / unit / union

The consonant **y** + long **u** sound is sometimes spelled using the **u_e** rule, where a single consonant appears between the **u** and the **e**. In these words, **e** is silent.

cube / huge / mute / costume / confused

There are similar **u_i** and **u_y** rules, but in these cases the **i** or **y** isn't silent.

puny / music / cupid / amusing / mutiny

The consonant **y** + long **u** sound is often spelled with a single **u** in a word with multiple syllables.

future / human / fuel / humor / accumulate

At the end of a word, the consonant **y** + long **u** sound is sometimes spelled **ew**.

few / spew / skew / nephew / curfew

At the end of a word, the consonant **y** + long **u** sound is sometimes spelled **iew**. This usually follows a **v**.

view / review / preview / overview

Unusual cases of a consonant **y** + long **u** sound include:

- **eau** like **beautiful**

- **ou** like **coupon**

- **ue** like **value**

Circle the word that best fills in the blank.

1. I'm sorry, but there is no _____ for what you did.

excewse / excuse / excus / excues

2. On this test, I made _____ mistakes than last time.

fewer / fure / fuer / furer

3. That's the only one like it in the entire _____.

ewniverse / universe / uneiverse / ouniverse

4. They will _____ that plan next year.

execewt / execut / execute / execuet

5. He is the most _____ player on our team.

valewable / valuable / valueable / valouable

6. Our teacher _____ our papers last night.

revewed / reviewed / revued / revude

7. We are stronger because our forces are _____.

ewnited / united / uenited / uneited

8. She felt so _____ that her face turned red.

hewmiliated / humiliated / huemiliated / houmiliated

THE SHORT A SOUND

cat / had / nap / fan / and

The short **a** sound is almost always spelled using a single **a**.

dad / ran / hat / pal / act

ladder / rabbit / backpack

Rare spellings of the short **a** sound include:

- **au** like **laugh** (**au** usually makes the **aw** sound)

- **ai** like **plaid** (**ai** is usually a long **a** sound like **paid**)

Compare the short **a** with similar sounds:

- **a** makes the short **a** sound in **cat**

- **a** makes the **aw** sound (like **saw**) in **ball**

- **a** makes the short **o** sound (like **hot**) in **father**

- **a** makes a sound in **ago** like the **u** in **circus**

different a sounds: cat / ball / father / ago

THE SHORT E SOUND

bed / egg / wet / nest / ready

The short **e** sound is usually spelled using a single **e**.

ten / bell / pet / desk / next

The short **e** sound is sometimes spelled **ea**.

bread / heavy / feather / health / pleasant

Unusual spellings of the short **e** sound include:

- **ie** like **friend** (**ie** usually makes the long **e** sound like **brief** or the long **i** sound like **lied**)

- **ai** like **said** (**ai** is usually a long **a** sound like **paid**)

- **ay** like **says** (**ay** is usually a long **a** sound like **play**)

- **a** like **any** (this letter **a** makes the short **e** sound)

- **eo** like **leopard**

- **u** like **bury** (compare with **fury,** which instead makes the **oo** sound)

Compare the short **e** with similar sounds:

- **e** makes the short **e** sound in **bed**

- **e** makes a sound in **item** like the **u** in **circus** (note that **item** doesn't rhyme with **them**)

- **e** makes a sound in **her** like the **i** in **bird**

- **e** makes the short **i** sound (like **is**) in **pretty**

different e sounds:

bed / item / them / her / pretty

Circle the word that best fills in the blank.

1. Be careful. The pan has a hot _____.

handle / hendle / heandle / haindle

2. You'll be fine. Just try to _____ in with the crowd.

blend / bleand / bliend / bleind

3. The _____ is really nice today. Let's go outside.

wather / wether / weather / waither

4. I don't have enough _____ left to lift those boxes.

strength / streangth / striength / streingth

5. Don't worry. Our dog is very _____.

frendly / freandly / friendly / freindly / frindly

6. Let's do this _____ tomorrow.

agan / agen / agean / again / agin

7. It's cold outside. I will wear my _____.

swater / sweter / sweater / swaiter

8. How _____ eggs would you like for breakfast?

many / meny / meany / mainy / miny

THE SHORT I SOUND

is / gym / built / women / business

The short i sound is usually spelled using a single **i**.

big / hit / this / stick / visit

The short i sound is occasionally spelled with a single **y**.

myth / symbol / rhythm / typical / physical

The short i sound is spelled with a single **e** in the past tense form of a verb that ends with **d** or **t**. In this case, the **–ed** ending adds an extra syllable to the verb, which is pronounced **id**. (Note how the words below sound like **hid,** and don't sound like **red**.)

folded / voted / tasted / graded / knotted

The short i sound is occasionally spelled **ui**. (The **u** is silent in these words.)

build / guilt / builder / guilty / building

Unusual spellings of the short i sound include:

- u like **busy**

- o like **women**

- e like **women** (and as mentioned earlier, the **–ed** ending for verbs that end with **d** or **t** makes the **id** sound, like **pasted**)

Compare the short i with similar sounds:

- i makes the short i sound in **is**

- i makes a sound in **bird** like the **e** in **her**

- i makes a sound in **cousin** like the **u** in **circus**

    different i sounds: is / bird / cousin

It is instructive to compare the short i and short **e** sounds in the following words:

    pin (short i) / pen (short e)

Circle the word that best fills in the blank.

1. Please, _____, would you help me find my dog?

mister / myster

2. Where did it go? It's a _____.

mistery / mystery

3. These _____ make rocket science seem easy.

womin / womyn / women

4. We still have a _____ of hope that it will work out.

sliver / slyver / sluiver

5. He _____ doghouses for a living.

bilds / builds / bulds

6. A pipe is shaped like a hollow _____.

cilinder / cylinder

7. Ants work _____ in their colony.

bisily / busily / bisuly

8. Do you remember what he _____ for dinner?

wanted / wantid

THE SHORT O SOUND

hot / fox / bother / calm / car / heart

The short **o** sound is usually spelled using a single **o**.

hop / rock / bottle / honest / constant

The short **o** sound is sometimes spelled using a single **a**.

This often happens before an **r** sound, forming **ar**.

far / art / star / carpet / argument

father / want / swap / calm

Compare the short **o** with similar sounds:

- **o** makes the short **o** sound in **hot**

- **o** makes the **aw** sound (like **saw**) in **long**

- **o** makes the short **u** sound in **from**

- **o** makes the **oo** sound (like **book**) in **wolf**

- **o** makes the long **u** sound in **lose**

different o sounds: hot / long / from / wolf / lose

THE AW SOUND

saw / taught / long / ball / talk

The **aw** sound is sometimes spelled **aw**. This often happens at the end of a word or before **n** (without **g**).

paw / claw / lawn / straw / awkward

The **aw** sound is sometimes spelled with a single **o**. This often happens before the **ng** sound.

song / wrong / along

The **aw** sound is sometimes spelled **au**.

cause / fault / launch / vault / sauce

Occasionally, the **aw** sound is spelled **augh**.

caught / taught / naughty / daughter

Rarely, the **aw** sound is spelled **ough**.

bought / brought / fought

The **aw** sound is sometimes spelled using a single **a**.

This often happens before an **l** sound.

call / halt / talk / wall / walk

An unusual spelling of the **aw** sound is **oa** like **abroad**.

Compare the **aw** sound with similar sounds:

- **o** makes the **aw** sound in **long**

- **o** makes the short **o** sound in **hot**

- **o** makes the short **u** sound in **monkey**

- **o** makes the **oo** sound (like **book**) in **wolf**

different o sounds: long / hot / monkey / wolf

AW AND THE SHORT O

The short **o** sound and the **aw** sound are two very similar sounds, yet they are a little different:

- The short **o** sound.

hot / fox / bother / calm

- The **aw** sound.

saw / taught / long / ball / talk

The following examples may help you hear that there is a slight difference. Compare these sounds closely.

lodge (short o) / long (aw sound)

hot (short o) / hall (aw sound)

calm (short o, silent l) / talk (aw sound, silent l)

calm (short o, silent l) / call (aw sound)

stop (short o) / strong (aw sound)

There are a few rules that help to distinguish between the short **o** sound and the **aw** sound:

- At the end of a word, the **aw** sound is more likely.

  saw / law / paw / claw / straw

- The **aw** sound is more likely with **ong** or **or**.

  long / song / wrong / corn / form

- A single **o** before other letters is likely a short **o**.

  hop / rock / bottle / honest / constant

- **aw, au, augh,** and **ough** make the **aw** sound.

  saw / cause / taught / bought

- **al** is more likely to make the **aw** sound.

  ball / wall / talk / walk / halt

Most words have only a single accepted pronunciation. For example, **saw** makes only the **aw** sound and **hot** makes only the short **o** sound. However, there are some words that can be pronounced with either a short **o** sound or an **aw** sound. Each of the following words has two different accepted pronunciations. For example, you can pronounce **dog** as either **d + short o + g** or as **d + aw + g.**

wash / want

dog / log

swan / swap

gone / golf

quality / qualify

soft / loft

Circle the word that best fills in the blank.

1. I was _____ when I heard that. I couldn't believe it.

shawked / shauked / shaughked / shocked

2. She works hard to prove that she _____ on the team.

belawngs / belaungs / belangs / belongs

3. The fireplace will help to _____ us up.

warm / waurm / worm / wourm

4. The _____ is circling high in the sky.

hawk / hauk / haughk / hock

5. Our dog was afraid of the _____.

thunderstaurm / thunderstarm / thunderstorm

6. Quit _____. We'll be late for dinner.

stawling / stauling / stalling / stolling

7. This dilemma has me feeling very _____.

distraut / distraught / distrought / distrot

8. Water is dripping from the leaky _____.

focet / fawcet / faucet / faughcet

THE SHORT U SOUND

cup / bus / ton / blood / trouble

The short **u** sound is usually spelled using a single **u**.

sun / duck / nut / shrug / bucket

The short **u** sound is sometimes spelled with a single **o**.

won / son / done / come / above

The short **u** sound is occasionally spelled **ou**. (The **o** is silent in these words.)

tough / double / enough / touch / country

Rarely, the short **u** sound is spelled **oo**.

blood / flood / bloody / flooded

Unusual spellings of the short **u** sound include:

- **oe** like **does** or **doesn't**

- **au** like **because** (**au** normally makes an **aw** sound)

Compare the short **u** with similar sounds:

- **u** makes the short **u** sound in **cup**

- **u** makes a sound in **circus** like the **a** in **ago**

- **u** makes the short **e** sound in **bury**

- **u** makes the short **i** sound in **busy**

- **u** makes the **oo** sound (like **book**) in **bush**

- **u** makes a sound in **burn** like the **i** in **sir**

different u sounds:

cup / circus / bury / busy / bush / burn

Circle the word that best fills in the blank.

1. Where _____ the cat like to hide? I can't find her.

dus / dos / dous / doos / does

2. The judge was well respected for his sense of _____.

justice / jostice / joustice / joostice

3. Unfortunately, I don't have enough _____ to buy it.

muney / money / mouney / mooney

4. My _____ visited our home last summer.

cusin / cosin / cousin / coosin

5. The show had already _____ before we arrived.

begun / begon / begoun / begone

6. We need a _____ to find our way home from here.

cumpass / compass / coumpass / coompass

7. My _____ won't feel well if I eat all of that junk food.

stumach / stomach / stoumach / stoomach

8. Too much rain causes _____.

fluding / floding / flouding / flooding

THE OO SOUND

book / foot / bush / could / wolf

The **oo** sound is usually spelled using a double **oo**.

look / good / wood / shook / outlook

The **oo** sound is sometimes spelled with a single **u**.

put / full / push / pull / sugar

The **oo** sound is occasionally spelled **ou**.

could / should / would

The **oo** sound is rarely spelled with a single **o**, like **wolf**.

Compare the **oo** sound with similar sounds:

- **oo** makes the **oo** sound in **book**

- **oo** makes the long **u** sound in **soon**

- **oo** makes the short **u** sound in **blood**

- **oo** + r rhymes with **more** in **door**

different oo sounds: book / soon / blood / door

Note: Not every teacher or author uses the same language or notation. If you are also using another book or if you are working with a teacher, note the following:

- Some books refer to **"long oo"** and **"short oo."**

- In this book, what we call the long **u** sound is the same as what others call the long **oo** sound.

  new / tune / moon / true / through / lose

- In this book, what we call the **oo** sound is the same as what others call the short **oo** sound.

  book / bush / could / wolf / cure

PRONOUNCING OO

The letters **oo** can make a variety of different sounds:

- The **oo** sound like **book.** This often occurs before the letter **k**, occasionally before **d**, and once in a while before **t.** It rarely happens before other letters. Exceptions include **wool** and **hoof.**

  book / look / shook / good / wood / foot

- The long **u** sound like **new.** This often happens when the double **oo** doesn't come before a **k, d,** or **t.** Exceptions include **food, tooth,** and **shoot.**

  noon / spoon / tooth / loose / choose

- The short **u** sound like **cup.** This is rare.

  blood / flood / bloody / flooded

- Similar to a long **o** sound like **more.** This can happen before **r**, but not always: **poor** makes the **oo** sound instead.

  door / floor

CONSONANT Y + OO

cure / pure / fury / furious / purity

Occasionally, the **oo** sound begins with a consonant **y** sound (like the word **your**) even when there isn't a **y** in the word. Compare the words in the example below.

sure (sh + oo + r) / cure (c + y + oo + r)

Note that the **y + oo** sound is slightly different from the **y + long u** sound.

cute (c + y + long u + t) / cure (c + y + oo + r)

few (f + y + long u) / fury (f + y + oo + r + long e)

The consonant **y + oo** sound is spelled with a single **u** and comes before an **r** sound, like **cure** or **pure**.

Note that **ur** usually makes the same sound as **ir** makes in **bird**. The consonant **y + oo** sound is rare: Common examples include **cure, pure, fury, furious,** and **purity.**

Circle the word that best fills in the blank.

1. He _____ by my side the entire time.

stood / stude / stoud

2. These seat _____ are really soft.

cooshions / cushions / coushions

3. You really _____ have broken that rule.

shooldn't / shuldn't / shouldn't

4. The notice is on the _____ board.

boolletin / bulletin / boulletin

5. The painting was hanging _____. I straightened it.

crooked / cruked / crouked

6. Your sofa is very _____. I might fall asleep here.

coomfortable / cumfortable / comfortable

7. The _____ you're looking for is standing over there.

wuman / wouman / woman

8. The traitor was accused of having an _____ heart.

impoor / impure / impour

THE OI SOUND

oil / boy / coin / avoid / royal

The **oi** sound is usually spelled **oi** when it doesn't come at the end of a syllable (like **avoiding**).

boil / noise / point / coiled / joining

toilet / poison / moisture / appointed

The **oi** sound is usually spelled **oy** when it comes at the end of a syllable (like **joyous**). The **oy** spelling also applies to plurals, like **toys**, and verb tense, like **toyed**.

joy / toys / enjoy / oyster / destroying

royal / loyalty / voyage / employee

The **oi** sound is rarely spelled another way. A rare exception is the word **buoyant**, where the **oi** sound is spelled **uoy**.

64

THE OW SOUND

cow / out / found / sour / flower

The **ow** sound is usually spelled **ou** when it doesn't come at the end of a syllable (like **pounding**).

loud / mouse / count / ground / scout

about / shouting / fountain / pouted

The **ow** sound is usually spelled **ow** when it comes at the end of a syllable (like **flower**).

how / now / allow / vowel / anyhow

power / shower / powder / brownies

The **ow** sound is sometimes spelled **ow** when it is followed by a single **l** or a single **n**.

owl / down / growl / frown / brown

Exceptions include **crowd, noun, foul,** and **browse**.

Rarely, the **ow** sound can be spelled like **drought.**

Circle the word that best fills in the blank.

1. He is very _____ to his teammates.

loial / loyal

2. I wish I had an _____ that could clean my room.

android / androyd

3. The nurse applied _____ to my rash.

ointment / oyntment

4. This show was provided for your viewing _____.

enjoiment / enjoyment

5. Try to _____ the ball as you run.

bounce / bownce

6. That _____ reminds me of an ice-cream cone.

cloud / clowd

7. With that bright shirt, you will stand out in a _____.

croud / crowd

8. Try to be brave. Try not to be a _____.

couard / coward

OW AND THE LONG O

The letters **ow** can make two different sounds:

- The **ow** sound.

cow / down / flower

- The long **o** sound.

own / show / bowl

The long **o** sound is more common at the end of a word.

For example, compare **grow** (long **o**) to **growl** (**ow**).

low / below / window / arrow / borrow / pillow

However, there are many exceptions. Following are examples with the **ow** sound at the end of a word.

vow / allow / eyebrow / plow / wow

Following are examples where **ow** makes the long **o** sound in the middle (or beginning) of a word.

own / bowl / known / shown / bowtie

PRONOUNCING OU

The letters **ou** can make eight different sounds:

- The **ow** sound like **cow**.

  out / found / our

- The long **o** sound like **no**.

  though / soul / shoulder

- The long **u** sound like **new**.

  you / group / through

- The **aw** sound like **claw**.

  cough / bought / fought

- The short **u** sound like **cup**.

  rough / cousin / young

- The soft **uh** sound like the **u** in **circus**.

  famous / nervous / serious

- The **oo** sound like **good**.

  could / would / should

- Part of the **ir** sound like **turn**.

  courage / journey / journal

The following words have similar spelling, yet make several different vowel sounds.

tough (short u like cup)

though (long o like no)

through (long u like new)

thought (aw like claw)

thorough (ir like turn then long o like no)

throughout (long u like new then ow like cow)

Many **ou** words have inconsistent pronunciation:

should (oo like good) / shoulder (long o like no)

cough (aw like claw) / rough (short u like cup)

dough (long o like no) / through (long u like new)

soul (long o like no) / foul (ow like cow)

soup (long u like new) / sour (ow like cow)

The best way to remember how to pronounce **ou** words is through memory and practice.

THE SOFT UH SOUND

a (a) / the (e) / ago (a)

item (e) / cousin (i) / carrot (o) / circus (u)

vinyl (y) / nation (io) / bargain (ai) / famous (ou)

The soft **uh** sound is actually the most common vowel sound in the English language. It is similar to the short **u** sound, but it is softer and weaker. The soft **uh** sound is very common in words with multiple syllables.

Every vowel (and even **y**) can individually make the soft **uh** sound, and some vowel groups can also make it.

ago (a) / item (e) / cousin (i)

carrot (o) / circus (u) / vinyl (y)

nation (io) / bargain (ai) / famous (ou)

We will consider the soft **uh** sound in detail in Part 3, which focuses on words that have multiple syllables.

Compare the soft **uh** sound with similar sounds:

b[a]ll (aw sound) / f[a]ther (short o) / [a]go (soft uh)

b[e]d (short e) / pr[e]tty (short i) / it[e]m (soft uh)

h[er] (ir like sir) / moth[er] (soft uh + r)

[i]s (short i) / cous[i]n (soft uh)

b[i]rd (ir like sir) / moth[er] (soft uh + r)

h[o]t (short o) / l[o]ng (aw sound) / carr[o]t (soft uh)

fr[o]m (short u) / w[o]lf (oo sound) / carr[o]t (soft uh)

w[o]rd (ir like sir) / m[o]re (o + r) / doct[or] (soft uh + r)

c[u]p (short u) / b[u]sh (oo sound) / circ[u]s (soft uh)

b[u]ry (short e) / b[u]sy (short i)

b[ur]n (ir like sir) / moth[er] (soft uh + r)

g[y]m (short i) / vin[y]l (soft uh)

r[ai]n (long a) / barg[ai]n (soft uh)

[ou]t (ow sound) / t[ou]ch (short u) / fam[ou]s (soft uh)

THE 'L AND 'N SOUNDS

There are two common cases where the soft **uh** sound is significantly reduced.

- **−le** and **−al** endings after a **d** or **t** (but not after the combination **nd**)

  title / cradle / little / middle / vital

- **−en** and **−on** endings after a **d** or **t** (but not after the combination **st**, where **t** is silent)

kitten / sudden / sweeten / widen / carton

Compare the sounds below. The apostrophe (') indicates a much abbreviated vowel sound.

cradle ('l sound) / able (soft uh + l sound)

middle ('l sound) / candle (soft uh + l sound)

sudden ('n sound) / ribbon (soft uh + n sound)

kitten ('n sound) / listen (soft uh + n sound)

THE IR SOUND

her / sir / word / turn / pearl

The **ir** sound includes a special vowel sound that is only heard before the **r** sound. Some dictionaries represent this sound with the symbol ʉ (which looks like a **u** with a bar through it) in their pronunciation keys.

Beware that many vowel **+ r** sounds are different from the **ir** sound:

were (ir sound) / where (short e + r)

stir (ir sound) / star (short o sound + r)

her (ir sound) / mother (soft uh + r)

word (ir sound) / more (o + r)

pearl (ir sound) / pear (short e + r)

The word **burner** makes both the **ir** sound and the soft **uh + r** sound: burner = b + ir + n + soft uh + r.

The **ir** sound can be challenging to spell because it is often spelled **er, ir, or,** or **ur.** There are a few helpful patterns. For example, **or** usually follows a **w** (but **were** is one exception) when it is pronounced with the **ir** sound (and not one of the similar vowel **+ r** sounds), and **th** is usually followed by **ir.** It's easiest to spell these words when you recognize them from memory.

per / term / verge / were / jerk

girl / dirt / first / third / birth

word / work / worm / worst / worth

fur / turn / hurt / burst / purse

Following are two-syllable examples of **er, ir, or,** and **ur.**

person / certain / observe / submerge / iceberg

dirty / thirsty / confirm / thirteen / squirrel

worry / worker / worldly / worthwhile

occur / purple / turtle / burglar / surgeon

There are a few exceptions, where the **ir** sound isn't spelled **er, ir, or,** or **ur:**

- **yr** like **syrup**

- **ear** like **pearl**

- **ou** like **nourish**

Remember that **ir** is just one of many vowel **+ r** sounds:

- The most common vowel **+ r** ending sounds like a soft **uh + r.** It is most commonly spelled **–er,** like **father,** which sounds different from **her** (the **ir** sound). For more about the soft uh **+ r** sound, see Part 3.

- When **or** doesn't follow a **w,** it usually sounds different from the **ir** sound in **work.** For example, **or** sounds more like the long **o + r** in **more.**

- The **ur** makes the **y + oo + r** sound in **pure.** Note the big difference between **pure** and **purse** (which makes the **ir** sound).

Circle the word that best fills in the blank.

1. The shot didn't _____ as much as I had expected.

hert / hirt / hort / hurt

2. The restaurant_____ free chips with every meal.

served / sirved / sorved / surved

3. Her job was to _____ the baton during the parade.

twerl / twirl / tworl / twurl

4. Unfortunately, your cough is sounding _____ today.

werse / wirse / worse / wurse

5. Hold the leash _____ or the dog may get loose.

fermly / firmly / formly / furmly

6. That speech was _____. I thought it would never end.

werdy / wirdy / wordy / wurdy

7. The company offered to _____ my mom's office.

fernish / firnish / fornish / furnish

8. I have a _____. What will the next test cover?

concern / concirn / concorn / concurn

VOWEL + R SOUNDS

You may notice that vowels tend to sound different when they are followed by the letter **r**. For example, compare **cute** with **cure** or **shape** with **share**.

- When what would normally be a long **a** combines with an **r**, the vowel sounds more like a short **e**.

  care / chair / their / there / bear / prayer

- When what would normally be a short **a** combines with an **r**, the vowel often sounds more like a short **o** (like the **a** in **father**, **want**, or **swap**). However, it can also sound more like a long **o**. For example, compare **car** (short **o**) with **war** (sounds more like a long **o**, rhymes with **more**).

  short o + r: car / farm / heart / sergeant

more like long o + r: war / warm / swarm / warrant

- Whether a long **o**, short **o**, or **aw** sound combines with an **r**, the result is nearly identical. Each word below sounds like a long **o** (for technical reasons, it is considered **aw**, but if you try to make the **aw** sound when you say it, it will come out wrong: try to say long **o** + **r** when you pronounce these words).

  more / for / four / war / door / roar

- The **ir** sound is a distinctly different vowel + **r** sound. This common vowel + **r** sound can be spelled many different ways, yet the sound is the same.

  her / sir / word / turn / pearl

- The soft **uh** + **r** sound is very common with words that have multiple syllables. The most common ending is **–er**, but it is sometimes **–ar** or **–or**. We will explore this sound further in Part 3.

  over / dancer / singer / doctor / collar

- When what would normally be a long **e** combines with an **r**, the vowel sounds more like a short **i**. However, note that the word **here** is often pronounced with a long **e** sound.

  ear / near / here / cheer / pier

- When what would normally be a **y + long u** sound combines with an **r**, the result is more like the **oo** sound. Compare **cute (y + long u)** with **cure (yoo)**.

  cure / pure / sure / furious / purity

- The long **i** retains the same vowel sound even when it is followed by an **r**. The long **i + r** sound is almost always spelled **ire** (one exception is **higher**).

  fire / hire / wire / admire / require

- The letters **our** can make multiple sounds.

  tour (oo) / sour (ow) / pour (o) / journal (ir)

VOWELS THAT OCCASIONALLY MAKE A CONSONANT W SOUND

one / once / choir

Rarely, the letter **o** makes a sound that begins with a consonant **w** even when there isn't a **w** in the word. Compare the words in the example below.

on (short o + n) / one (w + short u + n)

Note that the word **choir** is pronounced like:

choir = kw + long i + r

SILENT VOWELS

- Silent **a**

  pleasant / aisle / musically

- Silent **e**

  give / breathe / imagine

- Silent **i**

  bruise / business

- Silent **o**

  people / rough / colonel

- Silent **u**

  guess / guitar / laugh / tongue

Each word below is missing a silent vowel. Circle the answer that correctly fills in the blank.

1. cru_se

    a / e / i / o / u

2. hav_

    a / e / i / o / u

3. g_ilty

    a / e / i / o / u

4. he_lth

    a / e / i / o / u

5. le_pard

    a / e / i / o / u

6. ju_ce

    a / e / i / o / u

7. je_pardy

    a / e / i / o / u

1. Circle the words that make a long **a** sound.

   break / beach / obey / money / stayed

2. Circle the words that make a short **a** sound.

   champ / trail / weird / laugh / neighbor

3. Circle the words that make a long **e** sound.

   fry / deep / item / stream / were

4. Circle the words that make a short **e** sound.

   said / pin / behind / friend / ready

5. Circle the words that make a long **i** sound.

   tonight / city / retired / built / denied

6. Circle the words that make a short **i** sound.

   nice / list / try / guilt / find

7. Circle the words that make a long **o** sound.

   pond / double / prove / folded / roamed

8. Circle the words that make a short **o** or **aw** sound.

   soup / fog / gone / show / joy

1. Circle the words that make a long **u** sound.

   sun / do / fruit / view / beautiful

2. Circle the words that make a short **u** sound.

   son / fun / tune / cause / book

3. Circle the words that make a (short) **oo** sound.

   moon / blood / took / pull / would

4. Circle the words that make an **oi** sound.

   toy / paint / join / town / enjoyed

5. Circle the words that make an **ow** sound.

   cow / snow / taught / found / should

6. Circle the words that make a soft **uh** sound.

   away / full / famous / house / station

7. Circle the words that rhyme with **sir**.

   girl / form / were / turn / bear

8. Circle the words that don't rhyme with **sir**.

   work / fire / their / tour / term

PART 2

SPELLING

CONSONANTS

THE B SOUND

The **b** sound is spelled with a single **b** or double **bb**.

bag / job / tube / bubble / rubber

A word is usually spelled with a double **bb** after a short vowel when there are at least two syllables (or the past tense form of a verb ending with **–ed** with one syllable).

rabbit / hobby / ribbon / stubborn / grabbed

A single **b** usually follows a long vowel sound or a consonant, or when a word ends with **–able** or **–ible**.

able / ruby / noble / jumble / marbles

usable / terrible

A couple of exceptions include **rebel** and **trouble**.

The **b** sound is similar to the **d** and **p** sounds. Try to listen carefully so that you can tell them apart.

Compare big, dig, pig / Compare rib, rid, rip

THE P SOUND

The **p** sound is spelled with a single **p** or double **pp**.

pet / top / hope / happy / zipper

A word is usually spelled with a double **pp** after a short vowel when there are at least two syllables (or the past tense form of a verb ending with **–ed** with one syllable).

supper / puppy / ripple / clapping / dropped

A single **p** usually follows a long vowel sound or a consonant.

super / pamper / creepy / hoping / coupon (long u)

There are a few exceptions to these rules.

apart / proper / repellent / couple (short u)

The **p** sound is similar to the **b** sound. Try to listen carefully so that you can tell them apart.

Compare pig, big / Compare cap, cab

Circle the word that best fills in the blank.

1. Some students ride a _____ to school.

bike / bbike

2. A machine that resembles a human is called a _____.

robot / robbot

3. We _____ our hands together by the fireplace.

rubed / rubbed

4. We sat down at the _____ to eat our dinner.

table / tabble

5. A hollow tube is called a _____.

pipe / pippe

6. She _____ the tennis racket with one hand.

griped / gripped

7. He sprinkled salt and _____ on his sandwich.

peper / pepper

8. He wrote the answers on a piece of scratch _____.

paper / papper

THE D SOUND

The **d** sound may be spelled **d, dd, ed,** or **ld.**

do / did / side / daddy / riddle / spelled / could

A word is usually spelled with a double **dd** after a short vowel sound when there are at least two syllables.

ladder / hidden / muddy / saddest / puddle

A single **d** usually follows a long vowel sound or a consonant.

tidy / graded / folder / reading / poodle (long u)

There are a few exceptions to these rules.

holiday / ready (short e) / study (short u)

The **d** sound can be a little tricky. For example, the lowercase **l** is sometimes silent in **ld.**

could / should / would

The **d** sound can also seem tricky with some past tense verbs that end with **–ed.**

When you hear a **d** sound at the end of a past tense verb, the word usually ends with **–ed.** What can be tricky is that the **e** is silent (the **–ed** ending doesn't add a syllable) in many cases, like the examples below.

peeled / named / moved / cared / used

It's easier when the verb ends with a **t** or **d** sound (before adding **ed**), like the examples below. In this case, the **ed** makes the **id** sound as an added syllable.

graded / added / voted / started / dented

The **d** sound is similar to the **b** and **t** sounds. Try to listen carefully so that you can tell them apart.

Compare dug, bug, tug / Compare rod, rob, rot

THE T SOUND

The **t** sound may be spelled **t, tt,** or **ed.**

toy / cat / gate / pretty / sitting / hoped

A word is usually spelled with a double **tt** after a short vowel sound when there are at least two syllables.

little / butter / kitten / cutting / pattern

A single **t** usually follows a long vowel sound or a consonant.

total / tutor / rusty / waiting / straighten (long a)

There are a few exceptions to these rules.

water / city (short i) / patent (short a) / daughter

When you hear a **t** sound at the end of a past tense verb, the word usually ends with **–ed.** What can be tricky is that the **e** is silent (the **–ed** ending doesn't add a syllable) in many cases, like the examples below.

reached / laughed / cooked / trapped / fixed

Another thing that is tricky about the previous words is that none of them contain the letter **t**. Compare with the following examples of irregular verbs that actually end with **t** rather than **ed.**

bent / left / lost / went / built

Another way that the **t** sound can be tricky is when it includes silent letters, like the examples below.

two (silent w) / debt (silent b) / receipt (silent p)

subtle (silent b) / yacht (silent ch) / indict (silent c)

In the following examples, what may seem like silent letters are really parts of the vowel sounds. Recall that we learned about vowel sounds in Part 1.

right / light / eight / bright / thought

The **t** sound is similar to the **d** sound. Try to listen carefully so that you can tell them apart.

Compare tip, dip / Compare pad, pat

Circle the word that best fills in the blank.

1. It was _____ beneath the large tree.

shady / shaddy

2. The boy loves his _____ bear.

tedy / teddy

3. The toy cars _____ along the driveway.

rold / rolled

4. She _____ wait for her birthday to begin.

coudn't / couldn't

5. The book had a short _____ written on its cover.

title / tittle

6. The baby played with its _____.

ratle / rattle

7. The cat _____ for most of the day.

slept / slepped

8. We _____ on the icy ground.

slipt / slipped

THE V SOUND

The **v** sound may be spelled **v**, **ve**, or **of**.

vine / love / ever / movie / of

The **v** sound is often spelled with a single **v**.

van / very / evil / river / envy

When the **v** sound comes at the end of a word, there is usually a silent **e**. There is also a silent **e** in plural nouns where **f** turns into **ves**.

dive / move / gave / leave / arrive

rooves (plural of roof) / wolves (plural of wolf)

The **v** sound is similar to the **f** sound. Try to listen carefully so that you can tell them apart.

Compare van, fan / Compare save, safe

The word **of** is a rare example of an **f** making a **v** sound.

THE F SOUND

The f sound is tricky because there are several ways to spell the f sound, including **f, ff, ph, gh, lf,** and **ft.**

fun / life / offer / phone / rough / half / often

The most common spelling of the f sound is a single **f.**

for / from / leaf / safe / refer

A word is often spelled with a double **ff** after a short vowel sound.

off / stuff / coffee / muffin / effect

Two exceptions to this rule include **if** and **chef.**

The f sound is often spelled **gh** at the end of a word following certain vowel patterns like **ou.**

cough / rough / tough / laugh / enough

Some words instead spell the f sound with **ph.**

photo / graph / trophy / phonics / alphabet

A few tricky words have a silent letter with the **f** sound.

For example, the following words have a silent **l**.

half / calf / behalf

Compare with the following words, which are a little easier because they make a distinct **l** sound.

golf / wolf / shelf

The letter **t** is sometimes silent in **ft**, like the examples below (though **often** may be pronounced with a **t**).

often / soften

Compare with the following words, which are a little easier because they make a distinct **t** sound.

after / lift

The **f** sound is similar to the **v** sound. Try to listen carefully so that you can tell them apart.

Compare fan, van / Compare safe, save

Circle the word that best fills in the blank.

1. They _____ been very kind to our family.

hav / have

2. Please buy two _____ of bread at the store.

loafs / loaves

3. Remember to turn the water _____ when you finish.

of / off

4. The _____ has a long trunk.

elefant / eleffant / elephant / eleghant

5. She has a strong _____ that good things will happen.

belief / belieff / belieph / beliegh

6. The patient _____ several times this morning.

coufed / couffed / couphed / coughed

7. He only ate _____ of his sandwich.

haf / haff / half

8. We _____ walk home from school.

offen / often

THE L SOUND

The **l** sound may be spelled **l, ll, le, tle,** or **sl.**

like / tail / smile / tall / able / castle / island

The most common spelling of the **l** sound is a single **l.**

late / oil / rules / held / silent

A word is usually spelled with a double **ll** after a short vowel sound.

ball / silly / full / caller / smell

There are many words that end with **le,** which make the **ul** sound like **beautiful.** The consonant before the **le** is usually doubled when it follows a short vowel sound.

cable / riddle / title / shuffle / noble

A few words ending with **tle** have a silent **t.**

castle / whistle / wrestle

Rarely, a silent **s** is part of **sl,** like **island** or **aisle.**

THE H SOUND

The **h** sound is almost always spelled **h**. There are a couple of rare cases where it is instead spelled **wh**. The **h** sound always comes at the beginning of a syllable.

hat / home / behind / rehearse / overhead

The **h** sound almost always uses a single **h**.

hot / hello / hunt / behave / uphill

Rarely, the **h** sound is spelled **wh**. This can happen at the beginning of a word that starts **who**.

who / whom / whose / whole / whoever

Not all words beginning with **who** make the **h** sound. For example, **whopper** is pronounced with a **w**. Also, not all words beginning with the **h+o** or **h + long u** sounds are spelled **wh**.

home / hotel / hose / hold / hoot

Circle the word that best fills in the blank.

1. He hurt his elbow when he _____ down.

fel / fell

2. The orange had a thick _____.

peel / peell

3. Where _____ you eat dinner tonight?

wil / will

4. The papers were held together by a _____.

stapel / staple

5. Imagine what it would be like to live in a _____.

cassel / cassle / castel / castle

6. Wow! That is a _____ package.

huge / whuge

7. Her boot has a soft _____.

heel / wheel

8. _____ keys were left on the desk?

Hose / Whose

THE W SOUND

The **w** sound may be spelled **w, wh, u,** or **o.**

win / why / beware / penguin / one

The most common spelling of the **w** sound is a single **w.**

won / west / woman / flower / towel

Some words instead spell the **w** sound with **wh.**

what / when / while / where / whisper

The **k+w** sound is usually spelled **qu.**

quick / queen / quiet / require / liquid

Rarely, the **u** can make the **w** sound after another letter, like **penguin** or **language.** Also rarely, the **o** can make a **w** sound, like **one, once,** or **choir.**

The **w** sound is similar to the **v** sound. Try to listen carefully so that you can tell them apart.

Compare west, vest / Compare stow, stove

THE R SOUND

The r sound may be spelled **r**, **rr**, **wr**, or **rh**.

run / far / carry / write / rhyme

The most common spelling of the r sound is a single **r**.

red / bear / story / parent / smarter

A word is usually spelled with a double **rr** when the **r** sound comes between two vowel sounds.

sorry / current / worries / starring / mirror

Compare the words in the examples below.

story (long o) / sorry (short o)

staring (long a) / starring (short a)

The r sound is occasionally spelled **wr**.

wrong / wrote / wreck / wrap / wrinkle

Rarely, the r sound is spelled **rh**.

rhyme / rhythm / rhinoceros / rhombus

THE Y SOUND

The consonant **y** sound may be spelled **y**, **u**, or **i**.

yes / you / beyond / unique / onion

The **y** sound is usually spelled with a single **y**.

your / yo-yo / young / beyond / canyon

The **y** + long **u** sound is often spelled with the letter **u**.

Two exceptions include **you** and **youth**.

use / unique / usual / uniform / reunited

However, the letter **u** doesn't always make a consonant

y sound at the beginning of a word.

under / unlike / ugly / urn / up

In the word **unusual**, the first **u** sounds like a vowel,

while the second **u** sounds like **y** + long **u**.

Rarely, the **i** can make the consonant **y** sound.

onion / union / reunion / opinion

When it doesn't begin a syllable, the **y +** long **u** sound

may be spelled with the letter **u** or other vowel

combinations that sometimes sound like a long **u** (like

ew). Recall that we explored the spelling of vowel

sounds in Part **1.**

- Examples where **u** makes the **y +** long **u** sound:

    cute / accuse / confuse / excuse (noun)

- Examples where **ew** makes the **y +** long **u** sound:

    view / few

- Examples where **eau** makes the **y +** long **u** sound:

    beauty / beautiful

Circle the word that best fills in the blank.

1. The bird flapped its _____.

wings / whings

2. After it snowed the ground looked _____.

wite / white

3. Our hot dogs cost _____ dollar each.

won / one

4. We're running late. Please _____.

hury / hurry

5. Animals make spooky noises in the _____ at night.

forest / forrest

6. She sprained her _____ during the basketball game.

rist / rhist / wrist

7. The words whale and tail _____.

ryme / rhyme / wryme

8. He bought three _____ books at the bookstore.

yused / used

THE M SOUND

The **m** sound may be spelled **m, mm, mb, lm,** or **mn.**

mom / summer / thumb / calm / autumn

The most common spelling of the **m** sound is a single **m.**

miss / him / smart / camper / times

A word is usually spelled with a double **mm** after a short vowel when there are at least two syllables.

hammer / common / tummy / summary

Some words have a silent letter with the **m** sound. This happens with **mb, lm,** and **mn.**

limb / climb / thumb / lamb / tomb

calm / palm / autumn / column / hymn

The **m** sound is similar to the **n** sound. Try to listen carefully so that you can tell them apart.

Compare met, net / Compare came, cane

THE N SOUND

The **n** sound may be spelled **n, nn, kn, gn** or **pn.**

nap / funny / knee / gnat / pneumonia

The most common spelling of the **n** sound is a single **n.**

name / sun / rainy / pinch / banana

A word is usually spelled with a double **nn** after a short vowel when there are at least two syllables.

sunny / dinner / runner / tunnel / winning

Exceptions include **many** (short **a**) and **minute** (short i).

Some words have a silent letter with the **n** sound. This happens with **kn, gn,** or **pn.**

know / knee / knock / gnat / gnaw / pneumonia

The **n** sound is similar to the **m** sound. Try to listen carefully so that you can tell them apart.

Compare net, met / Compare cane, came

THE NG SOUND

The **ng** sound is a special sound that you hear at the end of a syllable. When **ng** ends a word, there usually isn't a clear hard **g** sound at the end of the **ng**.

ring / being / strong / going / moving

In contrast, when the **g** begins a new syllable after an **n**, it usually makes a clear hard **g** sound.

anger / hunger / finger / jungle / hungry

The **ng** sound is a little different from just a single **n**, and it's also different from an **n** sound plus a hard **g** sound.

long (ng sound, no distinct g is heard)

hunger (ng sound + clear g sound)

The word **tongue** also makes the **ng** sound.

NK AND NG

The **n** in **nk** actually makes the **ng** sound. You don't hear a clear hard **g** in **nk,** but you do hear the same **ng** sound that you hear in **ring** and **song.** There is also a clear **k** sound after the **ng** sound.

pink / bank / honk / think / skunk

Compare the words below. The left word ends with the usual **n** sound. The middle and right words both make the **ng** sound. The only difference between the middle word and the right word is that the right word also makes the **k** sound following the **ng** sound.

thin / thing / think

sin / sing / sink

sun / sung / sunk

win / wing / wink

Circle the word that best fills in the blank.

1. After studying, the test questions seemed _____.

simple / simmple

2. His teacher said that he needs to improve his _____.

gramar / grammar

3. Remain _____. We'll have the lights back on soon.

cam / camm / camb / calm

4. He straightened his hair with a _____.

com / comm / comb / colm

5. There were _____ people in the audience yesterday.

many / manny

6. She stayed up late last _____ to study for her test.

night / knight / gnight / pnight

7. He hurt his _____ when he punched the wall.

nuckles / knuckles / gnuckles / pnuckles

8. It took much _____ to lift the heavy box.

strenth / strength / strenkth

THE HARD G SOUND

The hard **g** sound may be spelled **g, gg, gh, gu,** or **gue.**

good / big / egg / ghost / guy / vague

The most common spelling of the **g** sound is a single **g.**

get / bag / begin / tiger / forgot

A word is usually spelled with a double **gg** after a short vowel when there are at least two syllables.

foggy / digger / biggest / nugget / rugged

Occasionally, **gu** makes the **g** sound.

guide / guess / guilty / guitar / disguise

Words that end with **gue** usually make the **g** sound.

league / vague / fatigue

Rarely, **gh** is used to make the **g** sound. (Ordinarily, **gh** usually makes the **f** sound or is silent.)

ghost / ghastly / spaghetti

THE J SOUND

The **j** sound is tricky because there are several spellings that include the j sound: **j, ge, gi, gy, dg, di,** and **du.**

jet / page / giant / edge / soldier / gradual

Sometimes the **j** sound is made by a single **j.**

jar / jump / justice / enjoy / subject

The letters **dg** often make the **j** sound.

wedge / ridge / badger / gadget / knowledge

The letter **g** is usually soft like **j** when it is followed by an **e, i,** or **y.**

gentle / cage / giraffe / allergy / region

Rarely, **di** and **du** can make the **j** sound.

educate / graduate / individual / soldier

It is unusual that the **g** in **margarine** makes a j sound.

Note that **d** is silent in words like **adjective** and **adjust.**

Circle the word that best fills in the blank.

1. That fly is really _____ me tonight.

buging / bugging / buguing

2. We are _____ to get started.

eager / eagger / eaguer

3. My mom parked her car in the _____.

garage / guarage

4. My dog _____ the backyard.

gards / guards

5. The boss _____ the suggestion that we leave early.

rejected / redgected / regected

6. The hail _____ the roof last night.

damajed / damadged / damaged

7. The _____ ruled that the man was innocent.

juje / judge / juge / jude

8. My _____ is really busy this week.

schejule / schedgule / schegule / schedule

THE K SOUND

The **k** sound is tricky because there are several spellings that include the **k** sound: **k, c, ck, ch, cc, lk, qu,** and **x.**

kid / cat / back / echo / talk / unique / box

One way to make the **k** sound is with a single **k.**

key / like / book / kite / monkey

Another way to make the **k** sound is with a single **c.**

color / class / arc / bacon / actor

The **k** sound may be spelled **ck** at the end of a syllable.

pick / snack / lucky / package / rocking

Occasionally, the **k** sound is spelled **cc** before **a, o,** or **u.**

raccoon / hiccup / broccoli / occasion

However, the double **cc** makes the **ks** sound before an **e.**

accept / accent

One common exception is **soccer,** which sounds like **k.**

Occasionally, the **k** sound is spelled **ch**.

chaos / ache / echo / school / chemistry

The **k** sound can be spelled **lk** with a silent **l**.

walk / talk / chalk / folks / polka dot

The **kw** sound is almost always spelled **qu**.

quick / queen / quiet / require / liquid

Rarely, at the end of a word the **k** sound is spelled **que**.

unique / antique / technique / picturesque

Here are two exceptions to when **qu** makes a **k** sound.

mosquito / turquoise

The **ks** sound is often spelled **x**.

box / taxi / except / complex / maximum

However, there are other ways to make the **ks** sound:

- A plural such as **blocks**.

- A verb ending with **s** such as **looks**.

- A double **cc** where the second **c** is soft, like **accept**.

There are a few rules that can help to spell the **k** sound:

- A hard **c** usually comes before **a**, **o**, or **u**.

  catch / corn / cup / local / helicopter

- The letter **k** usually comes before **e, i,** or **y.**

  keep / kind / leaky / donkey / making

- A word usually doesn't end with a single **c.**

  cook / dark / pink / task / break

- A **c** is more likely to come before **l** or **r.**

  clean / cry / crayon / scratch / bicycle

- A **ck** usually follows a single short vowel.

  black / truck / knock / rocky / stacking

- A **k** usually follows a vowel group.

  seek / book / break / awkward (aw group)

- A **kw** sound is usually **qu,** and a **ks** sound is often **x.**

  quite / question / fox / taxing / extend

Circle the word that best fills in the blank.

1. Last night we saw a _____ in the sky.

komet / comet / chomet

2. She ran five laps around the _____.

trak / trac / track / trach / traque

3. It was very _____ of you to spy on us like that.

sneaky / sneacy / sneacky / sneachy

4. I enjoy taking my dog for a _____ around the block.

wak / wack / walch / walk

5. They set out on a _____ for adventure.

cwest / kwest / chwest / quest

6. That idea would never _____ to me.

okur / ockur / ochur / occur / olkur

7. We solved a very _____ problem in math class today.

compleks / complecks / complex / compleques

8. My swimming coach wants me to work on my _____.

technik / technic / technich / technique

THE S SOUND

The **s** sound may be spelled **s**, **ss**, **c**, **sc**, **ps**, or **st**.

sun / toss / ice / scent / castle / psychology

The most common spelling of the **s** sound is a single **s**.

see / its / basic / system / serious

A word is usually spelled with a double **ss** after a short

vowel sound (but there are a few exceptions, like **bus**).

boss / mess / bliss / grassy / classic

The **s** sound may also be spelled **c** before **e**, **i**, or **y**.

race / icing / princess / dancing / bicycle

Occasionally, the **s** sound is spelled **sc**.

science / scissors / scene / fascinating

Some words have a silent letter with the **s** sound. This

happens with **ps**, **st**, and **sw**.

listen / fasten / castle / sword / psychiatrist

THE Z SOUND

The **z** sound may be spelled **z, zz, s, ss,** or **x**.

zoo / buzz / was / scissors / xylophone

The **z** sound is sometimes spelled with a single **z**.

zero / zone / size / crazy / prize

The **z** sound may be spelled with a single **s** when:

- the word is a plural form of a noun.

days / games / cards / kings / flies

- the word is a verb ending with the **z** sound.

is / runs / has / does / tries

- a **z** sound comes between two vowel sounds.

visit / losing / risen

A word is usually spelled with a double **zz** after a short vowel sound (but there are exceptions, like **wizard**).

buzz / fuzzy / puzzle / dizzy / blizzard

Rarely, the **z** sound is spelled **x**. This happens at the beginning of a word.

xerox / xylophone

The **gz** sound is usually made with an **x**. Note that **anxiety** is pronounced with a **z**, but **anxious** is pronounced with **ksh**.

exam / exact / example / exile / anxiety

Rarely, the **z** sound is spelled **ss**. This only happens in the middle of a word.

scissors / dessert / possess

Note that **possess** ends with an **s** sound. The word **possesses** is interesting because it has the **z** sound, then the **s** sound, and then the **z** sound again.

Circle the word that best fills in the blank.

1. Yesterday I planted a _____ in our garden.

seed / ceed / sceed

2. This is the best restaurant in the entire _____.

sity / city / scity

3. Would you please _____ the salt and pepper?

pas / pac / pass

4. This _____ been the best day of my life.

haz / hazz / has

5. I'm _____ at how well this painting turned out.

amazed / amazzed / amased

6. My friend was too _____ to play with me today.

buzy / buzzy / busy

7. He scored the winning point just before the _____.

buzer / buzzer / buser / busser

8. _____! That is the correct answer.

Egzactly / Exactly

THE SH SOUND

The **sh** sound is tricky because there are several ways to spell the **sh** sound, including **sh, si, su, ci, ce, ch** and **ti**.

shy / sure / special / ocean / chef / motion

The most common spelling of the **sh** sound is **sh**.

shop / wash / fishy / rushing / ashamed

At the beginning of a word, the **sh** sound is usually **sh**.

she / shape / ship / shut / shock

Rarely, a **sh** word may begin with **ch** or **su**.

chef / sure / sugar

There are several ways to make the **sh** sound in the middle or end of a word:

fashion (sh) / expansion (si) / tissue (su)

appreciate (ci) / machine (ch) / ocean (ce)

initiate (ti) / anxious (xi) / luxury (x)

Fortunately, many of the ways to spell the **sh** sound fall into patterns:

- **tion**: motion / action / nation / condition

- **tial**: partial / essential / substantial

- **tious**: cautious / ambitious / nutritious

- **sion**: tension / mission / passion

- **sur**: insure / pressure / insurance

- **sue**: issue / tissue

- **cial**: special / social / official / artificial

- **cious**: precious / delicious / gracious

- **cian**: magician / physician / technician

- **cien**: efficient / deficient / efficiency

If you can remember these patterns, it may help you spell the **sh** sound correctly more often. For example, there are many words that end with **–tion**.

Circle the word that best fills in the blank.

1. Your bracelet is nice and _____.

shiny / sciny / siny / ciny / chiny

2. A _____ of the students are really good at math.

fracshion / fraction / fracsion / fraccion

3. I never heard that _____ before.

expreshion / expretion / expression / exprescion

4. We washed our clothes in the washing _____.

mashine / matine / massine / macine / machine

5. I'm not _____ how to answer the last question.

shure / sure / chure

6. The large house seemed very _____ inside.

spashious / spatious / spasious / spacious

7. It was scary when the plane flew over the _____.

oshean / otian / osian / ocean / ochean

8. It felt _____ to spend the night at that grand hotel.

lucshurious / lucsurious / luchurious / luxurious

THE CH SOUND

The **ch** sound may be spelled **ch, tch, tu, ti,** or **te.**

chin / watch / future / question / righteous

The most common spelling of the **ch** sound is **ch.**

chair / lunch / inch / choose / church

After a single vowel, **ch** is usually spelled **tch.**

watch / catch / pitch / fetch / itch

Compare with words where **ch** follows a vowel group or when **ch** follows a consonant:

each / couch / bench / porch / teach

Exceptions to this rule include:

rich / such / much / which / enrich

attach / detach / spinach / sandwich / ostrich

Rarely, the letters **te, ti,** and **tu** can make the **ch** sound.

actual / fortune / culture / question / righteous

THE ZH SOUND

The **zh** sound may be spelled **s, z, si, ti, ge**, or **x**.

usual / treasure / azure / television / beige

The **zh** sound is sometimes spelled **su**.

casual / visual / exposure / treasure / pleasure

The **zh** sound is sometimes spelled **si**.

vision / decision / collision / occasion / version

Rarely, the **zh** sound is spelled with a single **z**.

azure / seizure

Rarely, the **zh** sound is spelled **ti**.

equation

Rarely, the **zh** sound is spelled **ge**.

garage / beige / genre / massage / sabotage

The word **luxury** can be pronounced with **ksh** or **gzh**.

THE TH SOUNDS

The letters **th** make two different special sounds. Note how the **th** sounds different in the first list below compared to the second list below.

the / that / father / this / there

thing / both / teeth / with / thick

Fortunately, both **th** sounds are spelled the same.

Another nice thing about the **th** sound is that there is only one common way to spell it.

Following are some more words that make a th sound like **that**.

these / bathe / breathe / those / feather

Following are some more words that make a th sound like **thing**.

thin / bath / breath / fourth / thirty

Circle the word that best fills in the blank.

1. During snack time I ate a _____.

   peach / peatch / peash / peatsh / peath

2. The chicken eggs _____ this morning.

   hached / hatched / hatshed / hathed

3. Would you please answer my _____?

   queschion / question / questchion / questhion?

4. I brought a _____ of bananas home from the store.

   bunsh / buntsh / bunch / buntch / bunth

5. My dad _____ my height this morning.

   meazured / measured / meatured

6. Our _____ is that our town needs a recycling center.

   concluzion / conclusion / conclution

7. We don't seem to have _____ that they would like.

   anyching / anyzing / anyting / anything

8. In math we practiced multiplication and _____.

   divishon / divition / division / divicion

C, X, AND Q

The **c**, **x**, and **q** sounds actually consist of other sounds that we have already discussed:

- The letter **c** usually makes the **k** sound, but often makes the **s** sound when it is followed by **e**, **i**, or **y**. When it is paired with **h**, the letter **c** usually makes the **ch** sound.

cat / ace / city / clap / cover / cry / cup / icy

- The letter **x** usually makes the **ks** sound, but can also make the **gz** sound.

box / fox / taxi / exact / exile

- The letters **qu** usually make the **kw** sound, but when a word ends with **que**, it makes the **k** sound.

quit / quick / quest / unique / antique

SILENT CONSONANTS

Silent b: comb / thumb / subtle / limb / debt

Silent c: scent / acquire / muscle / yacht / indict

Silent d: adjective / handsome / Wednesday

Silent g: sign / design / assign / foreign / gnaw

Silent gh: light / eight / bright / thought

Silent h: ghost / echo / chaos / school / honor

Silent k: knee / know / knit / knock / knight

Silent l: talk / walk / calf / could / should

Silent n: autumn / column / hymn / solemn

Silent p: receipt / raspberry / psychology

Silent r: February

Silent s: island / aisle / debris

Silent t: castle / listen / fasten / whistle

Silent w: two / who / wrist / wrong / sword

Each word below is missing a silent consonant. Circle the answer that correctly fills in the blank.

1. _our

> g / h / l / r / w

2. clim_

> b / g / l / n / p

3. cau_t

> g / h / gh / p / ph

4. _hole

> g / h / l / p / w

5. monarc_

> c / h / k / l / t

6. s_issors

> c / h / n / s / t

7. thorou_

> g / h / gh / l / t

1. Circle the words that make an **s** sound.

   pencil / pens / rose / nice / music

2. Circle the words that make a **z** sound.

   prize / desert / picnics / fries / xylophone

3. Circle the words that make a **k** sound.

   can / make / knot / race / unique

4. Circle the words that make an **sh** sound.

   super / station / mission / sure / vision

5. Circle the words that make a **ch** sound.

   chef / actual / action / fortunate / school

6. Circle the words that make a **j** sound.

   jar / angel / fudge / forgive / apologize

7. Circle the words that make a **g** sound.

   gear / gentle / girl / guess / cough

8. Circle the words that make an **f** sound.

   of / off / cough / though / graph

1. Circle the words that make a **j** sound.

jet / age / get / girl / college

2. Circle the words that make a **g** sound.

game / gem / give / laugh / guy

3. Circle the words that make a **k** sound.

cave / hike / nice / knee / antique

4. Circle the words that make an **s** sound.

was / race / fries / bacon / yes

5. Circle the words that make a **z** sound.

crazy / this / those / scissors / xylophone

6. Circle the words that make an **sh** sound.

push / sure / soon / television / mission

7. Circle the words that make a **ch** sound.

chapter / chef / scholar / fortune / actual

8. Circle the words that make a **zh** sound.

age / beige / range / vision / measured

1. Circle the words that make an **f** sound.

fix / roof / tough / though / thought

2. Circle the words that make a **kw** sound.

queen / question / request / unique / mosquito

3. Circle the words that make an **h** sound.

how / hour / what / why / who

4. Circle the words that make a **w** sound.

who / what / write / show / away

5. Circle the words that make a consonant **y** sound.

yes / bye / day / unlit / union

6. Circle the words that make a **th** sound like **thing**.

these / thirsty / bath / bathe / whether

7. Circle the words that make a **th** sound like **that**.

the / think / breath / breathe / weather

8. In each word, circle the consonants that are silent.

knot / calmly / straight / fastened / throughout

PART 3

MULTIPLE

SYLLABLES

SYLLABLES

If you can identify syllables, this can sometimes help with spelling. How? It's because many common prefixes and suffixes are used to form longer words.

re–place–ment

Consider the word **replacement**. The root of this word is **place**. You should recognize the word **place**. As a noun, a **place** is a specific location (like "the **place** where we first met"). As a verb, to **place** something means to put something in a specific location (like "please **place** the silverware on the table"). The prefix **re–** means to put back. When combined with **place**, we get the word **replace**, which means to put something back. The suffix **–ment** means the action or result of doing something. **Replacement** literally means the action of putting something back in its place.

pre–view

- the prefix **pre–** means before

- **view** means to see

- **pre + view = preview,** meaning to show before

quick–ly

- **quick** means fast

- the suffix **–ly** means in the manner of

- **quick + ly = quickly,** meaning in a fast manner

un–real

- the prefix **un–** means not

- **real** means actual

- **un + real = unreal,** meaning not actual

joy–ful

- **joy** means happiness

- the suffix **–ful** means full of

- **joy + ful = joyful,** meaning full of happiness

COMMON PREFIXES

Following are some examples of common prefixes:

- **re–** means again, like **refill** (to fill again)

- **pre–** means before, like **preset** (to set before)

- **un–** means not, like **unfair** (not fair)

- **dis–** means the opposite, like **disagree** (not agree)

- **in–** means not, like **invisible** (not visible)

- **ex–** means out, like **exchange** (to switch out)

- **mis–** means wrongly, like **misuse** (to use wrongly)

- **con–** means together, like **contract** (draw together)

- **anti–** means against, like **antisocial** (against society)

- **de–** means away from, like **deposit** (to put away)

- **ab–** means away, like **absent** (away)

- **inter–** means between, like **interfere** (come between)

- **intro–** means into, like **introduce** (to lead into)

- **bi–** means two, like **bicycle** (having two wheels)

- **tri–** means three, like **tripod** (having three feet)

- **semi–** means half, like **semiannual** (half yearly)

- **hemi–** means half, like **hemisphere** (half a sphere)

- **di–** means twice, like **divide** (split into two parts)

- **mono–** means single, like **monopoly** (single seller)

- **uni–** means one, like **uniform** (one form)

- **poly–** means many, like **polygon** (many sides)

- **sub–** means below, like **submarine** (under water)

- **super–** means above, like **superior** (higher up)

- **under–** means below, like **underline** (a line beneath)

- **over–** means above, like **overhead** (above the head)

- **para–** means beside, like **parallel** (side by side)

- **non–** means not, like **nonsense** (not making sense)

- **per–** means through, like **perhaps** (through chance)

COMMON SUFFIXES

Following are some examples of common suffixes:

- **–ly** means in the manner of, like **easily** (with ease)

- **–ous** means having, like **famous** (having fame)

- **–al** means relating to, like **naval** (relating to navy)

- **–ive** means characterized by, like **massive** (much mass)

- **–y** means characteristic of, like **messy** (like a mess)

- **–ful** means full of, like **beautiful** (full of beauty)

- **–less** means without, like **thoughtless** (no thought)

- **–ness** means state of, like **kindness** (a kind state)

- **–ity** means state of, like **reality** (state of being real)

- **–ic** means like, like **angelic** (like an angel)

- **–ish** means similar to, like **foolish** (like a fool)

- **–en** means to make, like **soften** (to make softer)

- **–able** means can, like **useable** (can be used)

- **–tion** means act, like **reaction** (act of reacting)

- **–ment** means act, like **agreement** (act of agreeing)

- **–dom** means state of, like **freedom** (a free state)

- **–ship** means state of, like **friendship** (a friendly state)

- **–er** means more, like **wiser** (having more wisdom)

- **–est** means most, like **wisest** (most wise)

- **–ify** means to make, like **unify** (to make into one)

- **–ize** means to make, like **realize** (to make real)

- **–ate** means to make, like **dilate** (to make wider)

- **–ed** means in the past, like **lied** (a lie already told)

- **–ing** means presently, like **running** (run now)

- **–es** means plural, like **boxes** (more than one box)

- **–or** means one who does, like **actor** (one who acts)

- **–ist** means one who does, like **artist** (who makes art)

- **–ology** means study of, like **biology** (study of life)

COMMON ROOTS

Following are some examples of common roots:

- **vis** means see, like **vision** and **televise**

- **port** means carry, like **portable** and **transport**

- **struct** means build, like **structure** and **construct**

- **gram** means written, like **grammar** and **diagram**

- **loc** means place, like **local** and **relocate**

- **vers** means turn, like **version** and **reverse**

- **sect** means cut, like **section** and **dissect**

- **form** means shape, like **formulate** and **reform**

- **lab** means work, like **labor** and **elaborate**

- **tract** means pull, like **tractor** and **distract**

- **log** means word, like **logic** and **illogical**

- **mand** means order, like **mandate** and **command**

- **voc** means voice, like **vocal** and **advocate**

WORD BUILDING

Many words with multiple syllables are built by adding prefixes or suffixes together with roots.

ex + port + ed = exported

- the prefix **ex–** means out

- the root **port** means to carry

- the suffix **–ed** means in the past

For example, **ex–**, **port**, and **–ed** combine together to make the word **exported.** If you put the separate meanings of **ex–** and **port** together, you get **export,** which means "carry out." If you add the meaning of **–ed** to **export,** you get the past tense, which is "carried out." The word **exported** actually means "sent to another country," which equates to "carried out" in the sense that goods are being carried out of the country.

Following are a few examples:

inter + sect = intersect

in + form + ed = informed

voc + al + ize = vocalize

con + tract + or = contractor

re + con + struct + ing = reconstructing

Beware that prefixes, roots, and suffixes occasionally change spelling when forming words with multiple syllables. When this happens, it usually helps the word sound or look better. Following are some examples.

- in + form + tion = information (gains an a)

- con + struct + tion = construction (two t's merge)

- re + vers + able = reversible (an a changes to an i)

- in + mobile = immobile (an n changes to an m)

- con + vers = converse (gains a silent e)

- ab + tract = abstract (gains an s)

Ordinary words can serve as roots, too:

color + ful = colorful

un + real = unreal

de + light + ed = delighted

Note that if you combine the meanings of the prefixes, suffixes, and root word together, the result may be somewhat different from the actual meaning of the word. For example, if you combine the prefix **non–** (meaning not) with the root **plus** (meaning more) to make **nonplus,** you probably wouldn't guess what the word **nonplus** actually means: "so perplexed that one is unable to speak." (However, once you know the actual definition, you may be able to see how it relates to the prefix and root. In this case, "not" + "more" means that you can't speak any more. In this example, the difficulty is that "speaking" isn't conveyed by the meaning of the prefix or the root.)

Note that prefixes and suffixes (and even roots) sometimes have multiple meanings. For example, the prefix **de–** can mean a few different things:

- In **derail**, the prefix **de–** means "away from"

- In **degrade**, the prefix **de–** means "down"

- In **defrost**, the prefix **de–** means "undo"

A prefix occasionally serves as an intensive, which means that it intensifies (adds strength to) the meaning. For example, while the prefix **dis–** means "opposite" in **dissatisfied** (which means not satisfied), the prefix instead serves as intensive in **disgruntled** (which means displeased and sulky, intensifying the negative emotion conveyed in a **grunt** rather than making it mean the opposite). As another example, the prefix **in–** means "not" in **inflexible**, but instead intensifies the meaning of "to lead" in **induce.**

1. Circle the prefixes in each of the following words.

confuse / displease / invest

absent / intercept / undervalued

bisect / envision / coauthor

introverted / unboxed / illusion

2. Circle the suffixes in each of the following words.

coastal / momentous / proudly

testify / energize / tasty

handed / messier / confrontational

friendliest / conditional / mandate

3. Circle the roots in each of the following words.

instruct / locate / portal

preschool / version / confuse

boating / booklet / interpret

acceptance / bimonthly / confirmation

destructive / transportation / automatic

Circle the word that best fills in the blank.

1. Class was so fun today we didn't want to have _____.

recess / ricess

2. My mom works for the _____.

government / governmint

3. My watch is _____ to me. It was a gift from my aunt.

precies / precius / precious

4. We spent an hour _____ about which option to pick.

debating / dibating

5. We walked together until our paths _____.

deverged / diverged / dyverged

6. That is the most _____ story I have ever heard.

fantastac / fantastec / fantastic

7. Do these exercises daily to help _____ your muscles.

strengthen / strengthin / strengthon

8. My dad _____ one hour to and from work every day.

commutes / conmutes / cormutes

COMPOUND WORDS

Two ordinary words are sometimes joined together to create a compound word. For example, the words **some** and **time** combine together to make the word **sometime**. Following are examples of compound words.

rain + bow = rainbow

book + store = bookstore

every + thing = everything

Occasionally, a compound word includes a hyphen (-) or a space between the words. The best way to spell these words correctly is to remember them.

ice + cream = ice-cream

up + to + date = up-to-date

merry + go + round = merry-go-round

living + room = living room

up + side + down = upside down

Break each compound word into shorter words.

1. firefly

   = _____ + _____

2. itself

   = _____ + _____

3. uphill

   = _____ + _____

4. forgive

   = _____ + _____

5. however

   = _____ + _____

6. someone

   = _____ + _____

7. noontime

   = _____ + _____

8. nonetheless

   = _____ + _____ + _____

TYPES OF SYLLABLES

There are several different types of syllables:

- Closed syllables end with a consonant. The vowel sound is usually short in a closed syllable.

pud|dle / mis|ty / be|gin

- Open syllables end with a vowel sound. The vowel sound is usually long in an open syllable.

pa|per / o|pen / hel|lo

- Silent **e** syllables have a silent **e** at the end that usually helps to make a long vowel sound. A silent **e** syllable may be a word, like **time** or **hope**.

com|bine / any|time / hope|ful

- Consonant **+ le** syllables end with a consonant plus the letters **le**.

a|ble / jun|gle / sprin|kle

- Vowel team syllables have vowels working together (sometimes with silent consonants) to create a single vowel sound. For example, vowel teams include the **ea** in **team,** the **aw** in **saw,** the **ay** in **play,** the **oy** in **boy,** and the **igh** in **night.**

laughter / today / famously

- Vowel **+ r** syllables have an **r** following a vowel. The vowel usually sounds different from normal when it is followed by an **r.** For example, compare the sounds of **car** and **cat** or **first** and **fist.**

army / doctor / regardless

Each type of syllable is based on the vowel sound. The vowel sounds offer clues that may help you spell a word that has multiple syllables. This doesn't provide a foolproof way to spell words, but the clues can be helpful sometimes. Let's explore how.

For example, compare the following two-syllable words. The words on the first line begin with closed syllables with short vowel sounds, while the words on the second line begin with open syllables with long vowel sounds. Do you see a pattern?

fas|ter / pret|ty / dig|ging / lon|gest / luc|ky

sha|dy / e|ven / pi|lot / ro|ses / tu|na

- When a closed syllable doesn't come at the end of a word, there are usually at least two consonants between the vowel sounds. Note how the double **t** in **pretty** and the double **g** in **digging** help to prevent the first vowel from making a long sound.

- When an open syllable doesn't come at the end of a word, there is often just one consonant between the vowel sounds. The consonant following the open syllable isn't doubled in order to help the first vowel sound long.

You can see this difference in the following examples. The word on the left begins with a closed syllable, while the word on the right begins with an open syllable.

din|ner (short i) / di|ner (long i)

hop|ping (short o) / ho|ping (long o)

sup|per (short u) / su|per (long u)

This doesn't just happen with double consonants (like **nn** and **pp**). The following example illustrates the same idea with **ck** compared to a soft **c**.

pac|king (hard ck) / pa|cing (soft c)

For similar reasons, there is often just a single consonant before the **e** in silent **e** syllables in order to make a long vowel sound. See the consonants **t**, **s**, and **c** that come before a silent **e** in the examples below.

re|late / sur|prise / nice|ly

There is a similar difference between open and closed syllables when they are followed by consonant **+ le** syllables. In the examples below, the word on the left begins with a closed syllable, while the word on the right begins with an open syllable.

bab|ble (short a) / ca|ble (long a)

lit|tle (short i) / ti|tle (long i)

gob|ble (short o) / no|ble (long o)

snug|gle (short u) / bu|gle (long u)

However, there are exceptions to these rules. Following are a few examples of exceptions.

hon|est (short o, n not doubled)

tri|ple (short i, p not doubled)

strol|ler (long o, double l)

mind|ful (long i, multiple consonants)

Circle the word that best fills in the blank.

1. I love the _____ on your dress.

patern / pattern

2. Those _____ are adorable. How old are they?

pupies / puppies

3. The event happened just _____.

recently / reckently

4. Please _____ all of the pages together.

staple / stapple

5. That was a really difficult _____ to solve.

puzle / puzzle

6. Will you be _____ in or out tonight?

dining / dinning

7. Please stow your _____ away before we take off.

bagage / baggage

8. My work has really been _____ up lately.

piling / pilling

1. Circle the closed syllables in the words below.

hotel / muddy / moment / facing / tangle

2. Circle the open syllables in the words below.

pages / bingo / dilate / music / return

3. Circle the closed syllables in the words below.

recently / beginner / hibernate / belittle

4. Circle the open syllables in the words below.

beginner / dependent / spectator / diversion

5. Circle the silent **e** syllables in the words below.

basement / retire / misuse / collide / telephone

6. Circle the consonant **+ le** syllables in the words below.

middle / angle / jingle / bottle / paddleboat

7. Circle the vowel team syllables in the words below.

because / awful / today / tonight / thoughtful

8. Circle the vowel **+ r** syllables in the words below.

razor / curtain / tractor / starry / report

STRESSED SYLLABLES

When we speak, we don't pronounce every syllable of a word with the same degree of stress. (If you did, you would sound odd, like a robot.) A standard dictionary uses a stress mark (') to indicate which syllables are stressed or unstressed. For example, in the word **person** the first syllable **per** is stressed, while in the word **forget** the second syllable **get** is stressed.

<blockquote>

per'–son (1st syllable is stressed)

for–get' (2nd syllable is stressed)

</blockquote>

We pronounce the stressed syllable a little louder and longer than the unstressed syllable. Pronounce these words and try to hear the difference in stress.

<blockquote>

fol'–low (1st syllable is stressed)

a–go' (2nd syllable is stressed)

for'–tune (1st syllable is stressed)

</blockquote>

The word **project** can help to illustrate the difference between stressed and unstressed syllables. That's because **project** can actually be pronounced two different ways.

proj' ect (short o, 1st syllable is closed and stressed)

pro ject' (long o, 2nd syllable is closed and stressed)

As a noun, the word **project** means "something that is planned and carried out." The noun form of project is pronounced with a short **o** sound, placing stress on the first syllable. The first syllable is closed in this case.

We're working on a class proj ect together.

As a verb, the word **project** means "to cast forward." The verb form of project is pronounced with a long **o** sound, placing stress on the second syllable. The first syllable is open in this case.

Use a device to pro ject the image onto a screen.

There are a few rules to help determine which syllable is stressed in a word with two syllables:

- Two-syllable nouns usually place the stress on the first syllable. Recall that a noun is a person, place, or thing.

moth'–er / mount'–ain / shov'–el

- Two-syllable verbs often place the stress on the second syllable. Recall that a verb is typically an action word (like run, call, or wave).

ex–plore' / trans–port' / con–fuse'

- Two-syllable adjectives usually place the stress on the first syllable. Recall that an adjective typically describes a noun (like red, small, or fast).

yel'–low / ti'–ny / grate'–ful

Note that there are exceptions to these rules. For example, the word **jin'–gle** is a verb that places stress on the first syllable instead of the second.

Stressed and unstressed syllables relate to spelling in a few ways. One way is that many unstressed syllables involve a soft **uh** sound (we will explore this in the next section). Another example has to do with single or double letters following a short vowel sound near the end of a word with multiple syllables. Examine the two lists of three-syllable words below. None of these words has a long vowel sound in the middle, yet in the second row of words there is a single consonant (instead of a double consonant) before the **–ing** or **–ed** suffix.

occur'ring / begin'ning / prefer'ring / recalled'

hap'pening / but'toning / tun'neling / doc'tored

The difference has to do with stress.

- When the stress falls on the second syllable, the consonant is doubled before **–ing** or **–ed**.

- When the stress falls on the first syllable, a single consonant comes before **–ing** or **–ed**.

Circle the word that best fills in the blank.

1. You weren't even _____ to what I was saying.

listening / listenning

2. Which object are you _____ to?

refering / referring

3. I participated in a _____ program last summer.

mentoring / mentorring

4. We have been _____ that story all week.

reteling / retelling

5. That was totally _____. It was a happy coincidence.

unplaned / unplanned

6. In the cave, the bears were _____ from the storm.

sheltered / shelterred

7. I can't believe that I _____ so many words.

misspeled / misspelled

8. Ensure that your seatbelt is properly_____.

fastened / fastenned

THE SOFT UH SOUND

ago (a) / item (e) / cousin (i)

carrot (o) / circus (u) / vinyl (y)

nation (io) / bargain (ai) / famous (ou)

The soft **uh** sound is actually the most common vowel sound in the English language. It is similar to the short **u** sound, but it is softer and weaker. Many dictionaries represent the soft **uh** sound by the symbol ə, which looks like an **e** that is both upside down and backwards. For example, the pronunciation of **banana** looks like:

bə–nan'–ə

The stress mark (') indicates that the middle syllable **nan** is stressed. The unstressed syllables **bə** and **ə** each make the soft **uh** sound, whereas the stressed syllable **nan** makes the short **a** sound.

The soft **uh** sound is called the Schwa sound, and is very common in words with multiple syllables.

politics = pol'–ə–tiks'

In the example above, the thick stress mark (ʹ) indicates the main stressed syllable, the light stress mark (ʹ) indicates a level of secondary stress, and the syllable without the stress mark is unstressed. The example below doesn't have a syllable with secondary stress: It has one syllable with main stress and two syllables that are unstressed.

syllable = sil'–ə–bəl

The soft **uh** sound is often heard in unstressed syllables.

The soft **uh** sound can be challenging to spell because every vowel can make the soft **uh** sound. If you can recognize some common patterns, that will help you meet this challenge. It will also help if you can remember common exceptions.

The soft **uh** sound is sometimes spelled using a single **a**. This is common at both the beginning and the end of words, as well as some prefixes and suffixes.

about / alone / away / ahead / again

tuna / comma / sofa / drama / yoga

machine / parade / dollar / woman / cereal

The soft **uh** sound is sometimes spelled using a single **e**. This almost never happens with the first or last letter of a word. It is especially common with **er** and **le**.

select / happen / over / couple / statement

The soft **uh** sound is sometimes spelled using a single i. This almost never happens with the first or last letter of a word. When the letter **i** is involved in a soft **uh** sound, it is often paired with another letter, like **captain** or **motion**, as we will explore later.

pencil / verify / identify / curiosity / heritage

The soft **uh** sound is sometimes spelled using a single **o**.

This is common with some prefixes and suffixes, like **or**.

It occasionally also happens at the beginning of a word.

p|o|lice / c|o|rrect / li|o|n / seas|o|n / idi|o|t

|o|ffend / |o|ccasion / |o|riginate / doct|o|r

The soft **uh** sound is sometimes spelled using a single **u**.

This almost never happens with the first or last letter

of a word (but one exception is the word **upon**).

|u|pon / s|u|ppose / b|u|rrito / cact|u|s / meas|u|re

Rarely, the soft **uh** sound is spelled using a single **y**.

vin|y|l / s|y|ringe

The soft **uh** sound appears in two very common words

that have just one syllable. The word **the** is usually

pronounced with a soft **uh** sound, except when it comes

before a vowel (then it may have a long **e**, like **the end**).

|a| / th|e|

When the soft **uh** sound comes in between other syllables, it is difficult to tell which letter is used. For example, it's very common to misspell **separate** (which has an **a** between the **p** and **r**, not an **e**). It helps to memorize these words. (The hyphens are shown just to emphasize how these syllables are broken down.)

mag-a-zine / cel-e-brate / hol-i-day

dec-o-rate / spat-u-la

The soft **uh** sound is sometimes spelled as part of a vowel group. For example, the common **–tion** ending almost always makes the soft **uh** sound. Following are a variety of examples where the soft **uh** sound takes part in a vowel group.

captain / ocean / foreign / surgeon / courageous

chauffeur / special / action / precious / genius

porpoise / curious / aqueduct / requisite

The following patterns, tips, and rules sometimes help to spell the **uh** sound. When a word begins with a soft **uh** sound, it usually begins with the letter **a**. There are a few exceptions, such as **upon** and **offend**.

ago / about / alone / around / appear

When a word ends with **uh+r,** it is usually spelled **er.** Words that end with **–or** often stem from words that end with **–ct** (like **actor**), **–ate** (like **calculator**), or **–it** (like **editor**). Words that end with **–ar** often follow an **l** (like **dollar**). Comparison words (like **smaller**) end with **–er,** even if they would follow the **–or** or **–ar** pattern.

dancer / singer / camper / player / smaller

tractor / doctor / alligator / creator / visitor

dollar / collar / regular / similar / popular

Following are some exceptions to these rules.

labor / favor / color / error / sailor / altar / liar

When a word ends with **uh+r+y**, it may be spelled **ary,** **ery, ory,** or **ury.** If you recognize that **y** has been added to a shorter word (like **nurse + r + y = nursery** or **treasure − e + y = treasury**), this may help you figure out the spelling. For other words (like **anniversary**), it helps to memorize the spelling.

summary / anniversary

bakery / mystery / nursery / pottery / machinery

factory / memory / history / century / luxury

Words that end with **ary** often make a long **a** sound instead of a soft **uh** sound. Compare the words below.

library (long a) / summary (soft uh)

When a word ends with **uh+n**, it is often **en,** but it can be spelled **on, ain,** or **ine** (but **sh+uh+n** is often **tion**).

open / happen / listen / fallen / given

gallon / lemon / million / bargain / medicine

When a word ends with the **uh+l** sounds, it is usually spelled **le**. However, there are notable exceptions where it is instead spelled **el** or **al**. Rarely, it can even be spelled **yl** (like **vinyl**).

apple / circle / handle / puzzle / waffle

shovel / panel / local / neutral / final

When a word ends with **uh+b+uh+l**, it may be spelled **able** or **ible**. In many cases, **able** is added to a complete word. For example, compare **readable** ("read" is a word) and **terrible** ("terr" isn't a word). Sometimes a silent **e** is dropped, like notable (**note – e + able = notable**), or **y** changes to **i** (like **reliable**). However, there are exceptions, like **probable** (since "**prob**" isn't a word) and **destructible** (since "**destruct**" is a word).

suitable / transferable / lovable / adorable

horrible / audible / incredible / reversible

When a word ends with **uh+t,** it is usually spelled **ate.**

Listen carefully: Words ending with **–ite** (like **granite**),

usually make a short **i** sound (like **definite**) or a long **i**

sound (like **excite**) instead of a soft **uh.**

estimate / coordinate / alternate / duplicate

Actually, the previous words can be pronounced two

different ways: When they are nouns, the **–ate** suffix

makes a soft **uh** sound, but when they are verbs, the **–**

ate suffix makes a long **a** sound (like **gate**).

Can you give me an estim⃞ate⃞? (soft uh)

Can you ⃞estimate⃞ the cost? (long a sound)

Some words with the **–ate** suffix can only be

pronounced one way. For example, **certificate** is only a

noun, so it ends with the soft **uh** sound, whereas

originate is only a verb, so it ends with a long **a** sound.

When a word ends with **uh+s**, it is usually spelled **ous**.

famous / studious / gorgeous / jealous / anxious

When a syllable sounds like **sh+uh+n**, it is often **tion**.

Occasionally, it is instead spelled **sion** (like **mission**).

There are also rare exceptions like **patient**.

motion / caution / portion / correction / rational

When a word ends with **sh+uh+l**, it is usually spelled

tial after a consonant or **cial** after a vowel.

partial / essential / residential / potential

special / crucial / social / artificial / official

Following are some notable exceptions to this rule:

initial / spatial / commercial / financial

When a word ends with **uh+ns**, it may be spelled **ence** or

ance. It's difficult to tell which without memorizing it.

absence / evidence / dependence / existence

substance / appliance / allowance / significance

When a word ends with **uh+nt**, it may be spelled **ent** or **ant**. It's difficult to tell which without memorizing it. However, note that **ent/ant** words often match **ence/ance** words. For example, compare **absent** to **absence** and **significant** to **significance**.

absent / evident / dependent / existent

pleasant / instant / significant / truant

In some of the cases where the **uh** sound is involved in a group of vowels, one of the vowels actually participates in a special sound. For example, the letters **qu** make the **kw** sound, **ce** and **ci** sometimes make the **sh** sound, and **ti** sometimes makes the **sh** sound. (We discussed these and other special sounds in Part 2.) If you recognize a special consonant sound with the soft **uh** sound, this may help you spell the **uh** sound correctly. Listen for the special sounds in the following examples.

patient (ti = sh) / **edition** (ti = sh) / **question** (ti = ch)

vision (si = zh) / **region** (gi = j) / **surgeon** (ge = j)

ocean (ce = sh) / **facial** (ci = sh) / **righteous** (te = ch)

anxious (xi = sh) / **acquisition** (qu = kw, ti = sh)

The word **rhythm** is unusual in that it makes a soft **uh** sound where there isn't a vowel. In this example, the soft **uh** sound comes after the **th** sound and before the **m** sound. It is pronounced with two syllables.

rhythm = rith′ əm

The soft uh sound can also be heard in some contractions, where an apostrophe (′) indicates a missing letter. For example, **doesn't = does not.**

isn't / hasn't / doesn't / could've / should've

Circle the word that best fills in the blank.

1. We explored the building from top to _____.

bottem / bottim / bottom / bottum

2. If you have an idea that may help, please _____ it.

saggest / seggest / siggest / suggest

3. Being a secret _____ sounds really dangerous.

agent / agint / agunt / agynt

4. I need to wash my _____ before the game tomorrow.

unaform / uneform / uniform / unoform

5. We saw a variety of _____ at the zoo.

animals / animels / animols / animuls

6. Little kids often do the _____ of what I tell them.

oppasite / oppesite / oppisite / opposite

7. Your words always _____ me when I'm feeling sad.

comfert / comfirt / comfort / comfurt

8. I met many of my distant_____ at the party.

relatives / reletives / relitives / relutives

Circle the word that best fills in the blank.

1. Are you sure that's the _____ way to do that?

propar / proper / propor

2. My grandfather is a stamp _____.

collectar / collecter / collector

3. I haven't played basketball since I got my _____.

injary / injery / injory / injury

4. Please help me _____ these two pieces together.

fasten / fastin / faston / fastain / fastine

5. What you did was not at all _____. It was too risky.

advisable / advisible

6. Did she _____ when the package would arrive?

menshon / mension / mention

7. I enrolled in a _____ arts class to learn self-defense.

marcial / marsial / martial

8. I have been saving my _____ for seven months.

allowance / allowence / allowince / allowonce

PART 4

SPELLING

HOMOPHONES

HOMOPHONES

Two different words that sound alike, but which are spelled differently, are called homophones. If you are familiar with the spelling and meaning of each homophone, this can help you choose the right word.

ate / eight

For example, the words **ate** and **eight** are homophones because they both make the long **a** sound followed by a **t** sound. Although **ate** and **eight** sound alike, these words have much different meanings.

- **ate** means the past tense of eat, as in "We **ate** popcorn during the movie."

- **eight** means the number after seven, as in "It cost **eight** dollars to watch the movie."

When a homophone is used in a sentence, you can tell which word is used from the context.

HOMOPHONE EXAMPLES

Following are some examples of common homophones:

hear / here

- Did you **hear** what the teacher said?

- My cousin came **here** to visit for a week.

blue / blew

- My favorite shirt is **blue** with white stripes.

- He **blew** his nose into a handkerchief.

right / write

- If you have a question, please raise your **right** hand.

- I need to **write** a letter to my parents this weekend.

sale / sail

- The store has a great **sale** on jeans today.

- The ship set **sail** yesterday.

ALMOST HOMOPHONES

Sometimes, two words sound similar, but not exactly the same. For example, consider the two words below.

picture / pitcher

- Please use my camera to take our **picture**.

- He poured a glass of lemonade from the **pitcher**.

Although **picture** and **pitcher** sound similar, if you listen closely, you can tell the difference: The word **picture** has a **k** sound before the **ch** sound.

picture = p + short i + $\boxed{k}$ + ch + uh + r

pitcher = p + short i + ch + uh + r

The words **picture** and **pitcher** are almost homophones, but not quite. However, they can still be confused easily because they sound very similar. When two words sound similar, it helps to see them used in context.

Try to hear the differences in the following examples:

flower / flour (flower has an extra vowel sound)

flower = f + l + ou + |uh| + r

flour = f + l + ou + r

- That **flower** is pretty and smells wonderful too.

- My grandmother likes to bake with **flour.**

pen / pin (e like beg, i like sit)

pen = p + |short e| + n

pin = p + |short i| + n

- I wrote a letter using my favorite **pen.**

- I fastened a ribbon to my shirt using a safety **pin.**

poor / pour (oo like look, ou like cough)

poor = p + |short oo| + r

pour = p + |similar to long o| + r

- They were too **poor** to buy things they didn't need.

- Please **pour** water for our guests.

COMMON MISTAKES

The following homophones include common words that are often confused. Study these words until you can remember the difference between them.

there / their / they're

- **there** means a place. "My house is over **there**." I could point to my house.

- **their** means belonging to them. "They can't find **their** car." The car belongs to them.

- **they're** means they are. "Do you know where **they're** going?" They are going.

Tips: Ask yourself if it would make sense to use the words "**they are**." If so, use **they're** with an apostrophe. Ask yourself if the word refers to a place. If so, use **there**. Ask yourself if the word refers to belongings. If so, use **their**.

its / it's

- **its** means belonging to it. "The dog wagged **its** tail." The tail belongs to the dog.

- **it's** means it is. "Do you know that **it's** time to go?" It is time to go.

Tip: Ask yourself if it would make sense to use the words "**it is.**" If so, use **it's** with an apostrophe.

to / too / two

- **to** can mean toward ("**to** the right"), on ("**to** the skin"), or until ("from one **to** three"), for example.

- **too** can mean also ("I have one, **too**") or overly ("that is **too** much").

- **two** is the number after one. "I have **two** shoes." I have a left shoe and a right shoe.

Tip: Ask yourself if it would make sense to use the number "**2.**" If so, use **two**.

your / you're

- **your** means belonging to you. "I love **your** hair." The hair belongs to you.

- **you're** means you are. "Do you know what **you're** doing?" You are doing something.

Tip: Ask yourself if it would make sense to use the words **"you are."** If so, use **you're** with an apostrophe.

sent / cent / scent

- **sent** is the past tense of send. "I **sent** a letter to my grandfather." I mailed the letter.

- **cent** means one hundredth, like one hundredth of a dollar (the same as one penny). "I can't even give you one **cent**. I'm broke." I can't even give you one penny.

- **scent** is a smell. "I love the **scent** of those roses." Those roses smell wonderful.

where / wear

- **where** means a place. "Do you know **where** my shirt is?" I want to know the location of my shirt.

- **wear** means to put on. "I like to **wear** my jacket." I put my jacket on.

principal / principle

- **principal** means a person in charge. "Our **principal** does a great job." The principal runs the school.

- **principle** means a rule. "The **principle** behind this is gravity." It obeys the law of gravity.

past / passed

- **past** can be an adjective meaning gone by ("it happened in the **past**") or a preposition meaning beyond ("my clubhouse is just **past** that fence").

- **passed** is the past tense of pass. "He **passed** the salt to me." Passing the salt is what he did.

Circle the word that best completes each sentence.

1. Be careful not to _____ the vase. It's precious.

brake / break

2. My dog runs in circles chasing its _____.

tail / tale

3. We're going _____ see a movie tonight.

to / too / two

4. I can't _____ you because the music is too loud.

hear / here

5. They found _____ cat in a tree.

their / there / they're

6. We flew across the country in a _____.

plain / plane

7. You should _____ that dress to the party.

wear / where

8. That is the best book that I have ever _____.

read / red

Circle the word that best completes each sentence.

1. I believe that _____ time for the show to begin.

it's / its

2. I'm not sure _____ way my dog went.

which / witch

3. The _____ is hidden behind the clouds today.

son / sun

4. We haven't gone _____ for a long time.

their / there / they're

5. My cat _____ seven pounds.

ways / weighs

6. They _____ breakfast just before we arrived.

ate / eight

7. I don't care _____ you walk or ride. Just come.

weather / whether

8. I hope I don't have to go to the _____ office today.

principal's / principle's

Circle the word that best completes each sentence.

1. I stubbed my _____ on the ground this morning.

toe / tow

2. I don't _____ who the twelfth president was.

no / know

3. Our cat got _____ claws stuck in the carpet again.

it's / its

4. We _____ like to take a vacation this summer.

wood / would

5. I finally figured out how _____ doing so well.

their / there / they're

6. My mother asked me to _____ milk at the store.

buy / by / bye

7. Are you sure? Those don't look like _____ shoes.

you're / your

8. We had our family _____ taken yesterday.

picture / pitcher

PART 5

SPELLING

PROPER NOUNS

PROPER NOUNS

A proper noun is a specific name for a person, place, or thing where the first letter of each word is capitalized. Following are a few examples of proper nouns.

- An example of a girl's first name is **Elizabeth.** An example of a last name is **Smith.** An example of a full name is **Elizabeth Rose Smith.** An example of a nickname is **Liz.**

- An example of a country is **France.** An example of a city is **Paris.**

- Examples of famous places include **Disneyland,** the **Sydney Opera House,** and the **Eiffel Tower.**

- Examples of companies include **Nike, Apple, Toyota, Coca Cola,** and **Amazon.**

Note that proper nouns begin with uppercase letters.

Proper nouns can be challenging to spell because many proper nouns don't follow the usual spelling rules. Following are some examples.

- The **h** in the name **Thomas** is silent. This name begins with the **t** sound (not the **th** sound).

- The word **Wednesday** is pronounced **Wenz–day.**

- **Nike** looks like it should have a single syllable with a silent **e,** but it is actually pronounced as two syllables with a long **e** after the **k.**

- The **Ju** in the name **Juan** makes the **w** sound and the **J** in the name **Jose** makes the **h** sound.

- The country **Qatar** doesn't have a **u** after the **q,** and the **q** makes the **k** sound.

We will explore a variety of common proper nouns which are difficult to spell.

TYPES OF PROPER NOUNS

Following are examples of proper nouns:

- A person's name, like **George Washington.**

- A location, like **Los Angeles, California, USA.**

- A geographic feature, like **Mount Everest.**

- Days of the week: **Sunday, Monday, Tuesday, Wednesday, Thursday, Friday,** and **Saturday.**

- Months of the year: **January, February, March, April, May, June, July, August, September, October, November,** and **December.**

- Holidays, like **Valentine's Day** and **Thanksgiving.**

- Book titles, like **The Lord of the Rings.**

- Store names, like **Amazon** and **Whole Foods.**

- Historical events, like **World War II.**

- Buildings, like **Empire State** and **Eiffel Tower.**

GIVEN NAMES

Following are a variety of common given names that are difficult to spell:

John (j + short o + n)

Anne (short a + n)

Sean (sh + aw + n)

Michael (m + long i + k + uh + l)

Stephen (s + t + long e + v + uh + n)

Thomas (t + short o + m + uh + s)

Hugh (h + y + long u)

Chloe (k + l + long o + long e)

Theresa (t + uh + r + long e + s + uh)

George (j + similar to long o + r + j)

Geoffrey (j + short e + f + r + long e)

Louise (l + long u + long e + z)

Leonard (l + short e + n + uh + r + d)

Miguel (m + long e + g + short e + l)

Jacqueline (j + short a + k + w + uh + l + short i + n)

Isaac (long i + z + uh + k)

Yvonne (long e + v + short o + n)

Raul (r + short o + long u + l)

Zachary (z + short a + k + uh + r + long e)

Naomi (n + long a + long o + m + long e)

Phoebe (f + long e + b + long e)

Penelope (p + uh + n + short e + l + uh + p + long e)

Jose (h + long o + z + long a)

Juan (w + short o + n)

Joaquin (w + short o + k + long e + n)

Jaime (h + long i + m + long e)

Xavier (z + long a + v + long e + uh + r)

Xiu (sh + long e + short oo)

Hermione (h + uh + r + m + long i + uh + n + long e)

COUNTRIES

Following are a variety of countries that are difficult to spell:

Afghanistan (silent h)

Azerbaijan (ai makes long i)

Belize (b + uh + l + long e + z)

Bhutan (silent h)

Chile (e makes long e)

Colombia (c + uh + l + short u + m + b + long e + uh)

Czech Republic (ch + short e + k)

Djibouti (j + short i + b + long u + t + long e)

Ecuador (cu makes kw)

Egypt (long e + j + short i + p + t)

Fiji (f + long e + j + long e)

Georgia (j + similar to long o + r + j + uh)

Ghana (g + short o + n + uh)

Guatemala (gu makes gw)

Guinea (g + short i + n + long e)

Guyana (g + long i + short a + n + uh)

Haiti (h + long a + t + long e)

Iraq (short i + r + short a + k)

Israel (short i + z + r + long e + uh + l)

Jamaica (j + uh + m + long a + k + uh)

Kazakhstan (silent h)

Kiribati (k + short i + r + uh + b + short a + s)

Kuwait (k + long u + w + long a + t)

Kyrgyzstan (silent z)

Liechtenstein (ie makes short i, ch makes k)

Luxembourg (our makes ir)

Malawi (m + short o + l + short o + w + long e)

Malaysia (si makes zh)

Mali (m + short o + l + long e)

Mauritius (ti makes sh + long e)

Morocco (m + uh + r + short o + k + long o)

Mozambique (que makes k)

Nauru (n + short o + long u + r + long u)

Nicaragua (gu makes gw)

Palau (p + short o + l + ow)

Paraguay (gu makes gw)

Qatar (k + short o + t + short o + r)

Russia (si makes sh)

Rwanda (r + long u + short o + n + d + uh)

Saudi Arabia (au makes ow)

Switzerland (z makes s)

Thailand (silent h)

Uruguay (y + oo + r + uh + g + w + long a)

Venezuela (zu makes zw)

Zimbabwe (ends with long a)

WORLD CITIES

Following are a variety of world cities that are difficult to spell:

Shanghai, China (ai makes long i)

Delhi, India (silent h)

Beijing, China (b + long a + j + short i + ng)

Mumbai, India (ai makes long i)

Dhaka, Bangladesh (silent h)

Cairo, Egypt (ai makes long i)

Seoul, South Korea (eou makes long o)

Bangkok, Thailand (not a distinct clear g)

Tehran, Iran (silent h)

Baghdad, Iraq (silent h)

Rio de Janeiro, Brazil (j makes zh)

Melbourne, Australia (ou makes uh)

Kolkata, India (k + aw + l + k + short u + t + uh)

Nairobi, Kenya (ai makes long i)

Buenos Aires, Argentina (bu makes bw)

Kiev, Ukraine (k + long e + short e + f)

Dubai, United Arab Emirates (ai makes long i)

Taipei, Taiwan (t + long i + p + long a)

Bucharest, Romania (ch makes k)

Kathmandu, Nepal (silent h)

Tijuana, Mexico (t + long e + uh + w + short o + n + uh)

Guadalajara, Mexico (gu makes gw, j makes h)

Kyoto, Japan (k + long e + long o + t + long o)

Prague, Czech Republic (silent ue)

Ljubljana, Slovenia (silent j's)

Ottawa, Canada (short o + t + uh + w + uh)

Phnom Penh, Cambodia (p + uh + n + short o + m)

Pyongyang, North Korea (no distinct clear g's)

Reykjavik, Iceland (j makes y)

STATES IN THE USA

Following are a variety of states (in the United States of America) that are difficult to spell:

Arkansas (as makes aw)

Connecticut (middle c is silent)

Georgia (j + similar to long o + r + j + uh)

Hawaii (h + uh + w + short o + long e)

Illinois (silent s)

Iowa (long i + uh + w + uh)

Louisiana (l + long u + long e + z + long e + short a + n + uh)

Massachusetts (e makes short i)

Mississippi (4 i's, 3 double consonants)

Missouri (m + short i + z + oo + r + long e)

New Hampshire (ire makes uh + r)

Pennsylvania (double n)

Tennessee (4 e's, 2 double consonants)

CITIES IN THE USA

Following are a variety of cities (in the United States of America) that are difficult to spell:

Phoenix, Arizona (oe makes long e)

San Jose, California (j makes h)

Louisville, Kentucky (l + long u + uh + v + uh + l)

Milwaukee, Wisconsin (double e)

Albuquerque, New Mexico (qu's make k's, not kw's)

Tucson, Arizona (silent c, long u)

Raleigh, North Carolina (r + aw + l + long e)

Minneapolis, Minnesota (e is long, o makes uh)

New Orleans, Louisiana (aw + r + l + long e + uh + n + z)

Wichita, Kansas (w + short i + ch + uh + t + aw)

Anaheim, California (ei makes long i)

Pittsburgh, Pennsylvania (silent h, double t)

Cincinnati, Ohio (three i's, double n)

Anchorage, Alaska (ch makes k)

Newark, New Jersey (n + long u + uh + r + k)

Lincoln, Nebraska (second l is silent)

Durham, North Carolina (silent h)

St. Petersburg, Florida (last vowel is u)

Norfolk, Virginia (silent l)

Chesapeake, Virginia (e, a, ea, e vowel pattern)

Hialeah, Florida (h + long i + uh + l + long e + uh)

Boise, Idaho (two syllables, long e)

Baton Rouge, Louisiana (r + long u + zh)

Des Moines, Iowa (two silent s's)

Bismarck, North Dakota (silent c)

Cheyenne, Wyoming (sh + long i + short a + n)

Juneau, Alaska (j + long u + n + long o)

Pierre, South Dakota (p + short i + r)

Montpelier, Vermont (ier makes y + uh + r)

PART 6

CHALLENGE

LISTS

SPELLING CHALLENGE

Following are suggestions for using these word lists:

- Study the words and how they are spelled.

- Ask someone to read the words to you. Spell your answers on a blank sheet of paper. When you finish the list, check your answers. (If you have the audio book edition of this book, the narrator will read the words to you in this chapter.)

- Practice writing each word several times. Writing can aid with memory.

- Look up each word in a dictionary. Write down its definition. Use it in a sentence. As you come to understand it better, you may remember it better.

- Make flashcards. For example, for **receipt**, you could write "a paper that you receive with a transaction" on one side and spell the word receipt on the other side.

LIST 1

easy

does

eye

menu

done

ghost

love

gym

edge

value

comb

attic

many

earth

LIST 2

suit

worse

gone

learn

chef

laugh

view

mayor

sign

rumor

clue

movie

awry

humor

LIST 3

would

again

guess

rough

pizza

ache

doubt

bury

sigh

castle

money

knock

bought

ocean

LIST 4

climb

fruit

ruined

thief

office

issue

people

loyal

nature

sword

bruise

prayer

beige

cereal

LIST 5

build

design

usual

thorough

juice

cookie

feud

canoe

sugar

vision

circle

memory

continue

guilt

LIST 6

library

knuckle

answer

science

cruel

social

friend

dolphin

neighbor

thought

urgent

ceiling

salmon

picture

LIST 7

unique

scholar

chimney

island

success

weight

mountain

auburn

traffic

column

delight

chaos

written

straight

LIST 8

beauty

species

plague

tonsils

stomach

plumber

journey

special

giraffe

fierce

delicious

country

diesel

grammar

LIST 9

align

weird

bayou

fiery

naïve

either

juror

height

harass

believe

license

squirrel

penguin

refugee

LIST 10

league

acquit

foreign

occurred

receive

jewelry

foliage

pharaoh

sergeant

success

gracious

avenue

tyranny

ambulance

LIST 11

acquire

apparent

accident

schedule

larynx

parallel

beverage

restaurant

temperature

maneuver

available

suspicion

boulevard

paraphernalia

LIST 12

cemetery

guarantee

conscience

discipline

playwright

embarrass

catastrophe

surveillance

handkerchief

mischievous

convalescent

idiosyncrasy

questionnaire

chrysanthemum

LIST 13

biscuit

satchel

leopard

scissors

massage

precious

subtle

receipt

neutral

colonel

relevant

persuade

separate

campaign

LIST 14

guitar

rhythm

agility

physics

fragile

orchard

jeopardy

spaghetti

misspelled

language

knickknack

medicine

mosquito

rhinoceros

LIST 15

independence

frivolous

exaggerated

facilitator

inheritance

ridiculous

eventually

unacceptable

fictitious

extraneous

uncomfortable

indispensable

overabundant

extraordinarily

LIST 16

algae

radii

fjord

llama

aorta

psychic

gauge

aerobic

chauffeur

vacuum

iridescent

aardvark

pneumonia

pharmaceutical

APPENDIX

TECHNICAL

TERMS

TERMINOLOGY

Until now, we have avoided using technical jargon in order to help make the concepts clear to everybody, regardless of their background. If you're reading a spelling or phonics book, but aren't familiar with words like diphthong or Schwa, this new vocabulary can add to the challenge of trying to understand the main ideas. On the other hand, if you learn this vocabulary, this will be helpful if:

- You read a book or online article about spelling or phonics that uses technical terms.

- You work with an instructor or tutor. If you and the instructor both know the terminology, you can communicate more precisely about phonics.

- You discuss ideas with other students who are familiar with the terminology.

digraph: a pair of letters that represents a single sound, like **ph**, **ou**, or **ck**.

diphthong: a combined vowel sound that begins as one vowel and ends as another vowel. Some common diphthongs include:

- the **au** diphthong: the **ou** in **cloud** or **brown**

- the **oi** diphthong: the **oi** in **noise** or **boy**

- the **ou** diphthong: the long **a** in **rain** or **plane**

- the **ai** diphthong: the long **i** in **right** or **bite**

- the **ei** diphthong: the long **o** in **road** or **no**

Note that **diphthongs** refer to how you make the vowel sound with your mouth (not how you spell the word). Although some diphthongs are spelled with a pair of vowels (like **cloud**), many are not (like **ride**). In comparison, a digraph is pair of letters (like **sh** or **ou**) that make a single sound.

phoneme: a single individual sound, like **f** or **t.**

grapheme: one or more letters that represent a single phoneme, like **b, ch,** or **igh.** For example, the graphemes **f, ph,** and **gh** correspond to the phoneme **f** (since **f, ph,** and **gh** can each make the **f** sound).

blend: separate sounds that are put together, like **ct** or **fr,** where you can still hear the individual phonemes.

r-controlled vowel: a vowel that sounds a little different before an **r.** Compare **shape** with **share.**

onset: the initial consonant sounds of a syllable, like the **cl** in **clap** or the **r** in **rain.**

rime: the vowel sound plus any following consonant sounds of a syllable, like the **ap** in **clap** or the **ou** in **you.** For example, in the word **shown,** the onset is **sh** and the rime is **own.**

Schwa: the soft **uh** sound that is commonly heard in unstressed syllables of multi-syllable words. Examples include the **a** in **ago**, the **e** in **item**, the **i** in **cousin**, the **o** in **carrot**, and the **u** in **circus**. The Schwa sound is represented by the symbol **ə**, which looks like an **e** that is both upside down and backwards.

SYMBOLS

ā, ē, ī, ō, and ū: long vowel sounds.

ä: the short **o** sound, like **hot** and the **a** in **father**.

ô: the **aw** sound, like **saw** and **long**.

oo: the (short) **oo** sound, like **book** and **put**.

o̅o̅: the long **u** sound, like **moon** and **tune**. It's the same

as what we have called ū (the long **u**) in this book.

ʉ: the vowel in the **ir** sound, like **sir** and **her**.

ə: the Schwa symbol, like the **a** in **ago**.

ŋ: the **ng** sound that doesn't make a clear distinct **g**, like

ring and **being**. You also hear it in **pink** before the **k**.

th: the **th** sound like **the** and **that**.

th: the **th** sound like **thin** and **thing**.

ANSWER KEY

Part 1

Page 17

1. fine (note: the meaning of fin doesn't fit the context)
2. pal (note: the meaning of pale doesn't fit the context)
3. slope (note: the meaning of slop doesn't fit the context)
4. scrap (note: the meaning of scrape doesn't fit the context)
5. airplane
6. include
7. hoping
8. shady (note: the meaning of shade doesn't fit the context)

Page 21

1. scraped
2. tray
3. chasing
4. train
5. eighty
6. shake
7. stranger
8. strayed

Page 25

1. jeans
2. green
3. athlete
4. lucky
5. piece (note: the meaning of peace doesn't fit the context)
6. received
7. refused
8. chimney

Page 28

1. deny
2. might (note: the meaning of mite doesn't fit the context)
3. ripe
4. blind
5. tidy
6. applied
7. silent
8. buy (note: the meaning of by and bye don't fit the context)

Page 31

1. ceiling
2. supplies
3. deceiving
4. belief
5. pier
6. neighborhood
7. scientific
8. neither

Page 35

1. broken
2. borrow
3. float
4. bowl
5. focus
6. told
7. throat
8. shoulder

Page 38

1. knew
2. lunatic
3. cartoons
4. ruler
5. routine
6. juicy
7. shoes
8. rescued

Page 41

1. excuse
2. fewer
3. universe
4. execute
5. valuable
6. reviewed
7. united
8. humiliated

Page 45

1. handle
2. blend
3. weather
4. strength
5. friendly
6. again
7. sweater
8. many

Page 48

1. mister
2. mystery
3. women
4. sliver
5. builds
6. cylinder
7. busily
8. wanted

Page 55

1. shocked
2. belongs
3. warm (note: the meaning of worm doesn't fit the context)
4. hawk (note: the meaning of hock doesn't fit the context)
5. thunderstorm
6. stalling
7. distraught
8. faucet

Page 58

1. does
2. justice
3. money
4. cousin
5. begun
6. compass
7. stomach
8. flooding

Page 63

1. stood
2. cushions
3. shouldn't
4. bulletin
5. crooked
6. comfortable
7. woman
8. impure

Page 66

1. loyal
2. android
3. ointment
4. enjoyment
5. bounce
6. cloud
7. crowd
8. coward

Page 76

1. hurt
2. served
3. twirl
4. worse
5. firmly
6. wordy
7. furnish
8. concern

Page 82
1. i (cruise)
2. e (have)
3. u (guilty)
4. a (health)
5. o (leopard)
6. i (juice)
7. o (jeopardy)

Page 83
1. break, obey, stayed
2. champ, laugh

   (trail/neighbor make long **a**)
3. deep, stream
4. said, friend, ready

   (pin makes short **i**, unlike pen;

   behind makes long **e** and long **i**)
5. tonight, retired, denied

   (city/built make short **i**)
6. list, guilt

   (the others make long **i**)
7. folded, roamed
8. fog, gone

Page 84
1. do, fruit, view, beautiful
2. son, fun

   (book makes the short **oo** sound)
3. took, pull, would

   (moon makes long **u**,

   blood makes short **u**)
4. toy, join, enjoyed
5. cow, found
6. away, famous, station

   (full makes short **u**)
7. girl, were, turn
8. fire, their, tour

Part 2

Page 88
1. bike
2. robot
3. rubbed
4. table
5. pipe
6. gripped
7. pepper
8. paper

Page 93
1. shady
2. teddy
3. rolled
4. couldn't
5. title
6. rattle
7. slept
8. slipped

Page 97
1. have
2. loaves
3. off (note: both are real words, but only off fits the context)
4. elephant
5. belief
6. coughed
7. half
8. often

Page 100
1. fell
2. peel
3. will
4. staple
5. castle
6. huge
7. heel (note: the meaning of wheel doesn't fit the context)
8. Whose (note: the meaning of hose doesn't fit the context)

Page 105
1. wings
2. white
3. one (note: the meaning of won doesn't fit the context)
4. hurry
5. forest
6. wrist
7. rhyme
8. used

Page 110
1. simple
2. grammar
3. calm
4. comb
5. many
6. night (note: the meaning of knight doesn't fit the context)
7. knuckles
8. strength

Page 113
1. bugging
2. eager
3. garage
4. guards
5. rejected
6. damaged
7. judge
8. schedule

Page 117
1. comet
2. track
3. sneaky
4. walk
5. quest
6. occur
7. complex
8. technique

Page 121
1. seed
2. city
3. pass
4. has
5. amazed
6. busy
7. buzzer
8. Exactly

Page 124
1. shiny
2. fraction
3. expression
4. machine
5. sure
6. spacious
7. ocean
8. luxurious

Page 128
1. peach
2. hatched
3. question
4. bunch
5. measured
6. conclusion
7. anything
8. division

Page 131
1. h (hour)
2. b (climb)
3. gh (caught)
4. w (whole)
5. h (monarch)
6. c (scissors)
7. gh (thorough)

Page 132

1. pencil, nice

   (the others make a **z** sound)
2. prize, desert, fries, xylophone

   (picnics makes an **s** sound)
3. can, make, unique
4. station, mission, sure

   (vision makes a **zh** sound)
5. actual, fortunate

   (chef and action make an **sh**

   sound; school makes a **k** sound)
6. jar, angel, fudge, apologize
7. gear, girl, guess

   (gentle makes a **j** sound;

   cough makes an **f** sound)
8. off, cough, graph

   (of makes a **v** sound;

   gh is silent in though)

Page 133

1. jet, age, college
2. game, give, guy

   (gem makes a **j** sound;

   laugh makes an **f** sound)
3. cave, hike, antique
4. race, yes

   (was and fries make **z** sounds)
5. crazy, those, scissors,

   xylophone (the **ss** and ending of

   scissors both make **z** sounds)
6. push, sure, mission

   (television makes a **zh** sound)
7. chapter, fortune, actual

   (chef makes an **sh** sound;

   scholar makes a **k** sound)
8. beige, vision, measured

   (the others make **j** sounds)

Page 134

1. fix, roof, tough

   (the **gh** is silent in though and

   thought)
2. queen, question, request

   (the others make a **k** sound)
3. how, who

   (**h** is silent in hour;

   what and why make **w** sounds)
4. what, away

   (who makes an **h** sound;

   write makes an **r** sound;

   ow makes a long **o** in show)
5. yes, union
6. thirsty, bath
7. the, breathe, weather
8. n (k[n]ot), l (ca[l]mly),

   gh (strai[gh]t), t (fas[t]ened),

   gh (throu[gh]out)

Part 3

Page 147

1. con / dis / in

   ab / inter / under

   bi / en / co

   intro / un / il
2. al / ous / ly

   ify / ize / y

   ed / ier / ational (a + tion + al)

   liest (li + est) / itional (i + tion

   + al) / ate
3. struct / loc / port

   school / vers / fuse

   boat / book / pret

   cept / month / firm

   struct / port / mat

Page 148
1. recess
2. government
3. precious
4. debating
5. diverged
6. fantastic
7. strengthen
8. commutes

Page 150
1. fire + fly
2. it + self
3. up + hill
4. for + give
5. how + ever
6. some + one
7. noon + time
8. none + the + less

Page 156
1. pattern
2. puppies
3. recently
4. staple
5. puzzle
6. dining
7. baggage
8. piling

Page 157
1. tel / mud / ment / cing / tan
2. pa / go / di / mu / re
3. cent / gin + ner / ber / lit
4. be / de / ta / di
5. base / tire / use / lide / phone (the **e** in tele isn't silent)
6. dle / gle / gle / tle / dle
7. cause / aw / day / night / thought
8. zor / cur / tor / star / port

Page 162
1. listening
2. referring
3. mentoring
4. retelling
5. unplanned
6. sheltered
7. misspelled
8. fastened

Page 175
1. bottom
2. suggest
3. agent
4. uniform
5. animals
6. opposite
7. comfort
8. relatives

Page 176
1. proper
2. collector
3. injury
4. fasten
5. advisable
6. mention
7. martial
8. allowance

Part 4
Page 186
1. break (since break results in damage, whereas brake means to slow down)
2. tail (since animals have a tail, whereas tale is a story)
3. to (since the preposition "to" best fits in the blank, whereas too – meaning "also" – and two – the number 2 – wouldn't make sense)

4. hear (since hear is what you do with your ear, whereas here means this place)
5. their (since the cat belongs to them, whereas there – a place – and they're – they are – wouldn't make sense)
6. plane (since you fly in a plane, whereas plain means open, basic, or undecorated)
7. wear (since you wear clothes, whereas "where" is a place)
8. read (since this is the past tense of read, whereas red is a color)

Page 187
1. it's (since you could write "it is" in the blank instead, whereas "its" has a sense of belonging)
2. which (since which refers to one of the possible directions, whereas a witch casts spells)
3. sun (since we see a sun in the sky during the day, whereas a son is a parent's male child)
4. there (since there refers to a place, whereas their has a sense of belonging and they're means they are)
5. weighs (since weigh refers to how heavy the cat is, whereas way is a path or direction)
6. ate (since ate is the past tense of eat, whereas eight is a number)
7. whether (since whether refers to a choice, whereas weather refers to things like rain, snow, clouds, or sunshine)
8. principal's (since principal is a person in charge, whereas principle is a rule)

Page 188
1. toe (since toe is a part of a foot, whereas tow means to pull something along like a car)
2. know (since know refers to something that you have learned, whereas no is the opposite of yes)
3. its (since its refers to the claws that belong to the cat, whereas it's doesn't work because it wouldn't make sense to write "it is" in the blank)
4. would (since the alternative, wood, doesn't make sense, because wood is a substance that comes from a tree)
5. they're (since it would make sense to write "they are" in the blank)
6. buy (since buy refers to a purchase, whereas the preposition by and the word bye – as in goodbye – wouldn't make sense)
7. your (since the shoes belong to you, whereas it wouldn't make sense to write "you are" in the blank)
8. picture (since a picture is taken with a camera, whereas you pour liquid from a pitcher)

INDEX

A

a (long) 18-21

a (making aw sound) 51

a (making short e) 43

a (making short o) 49

a (making uh sound) 70, 165, 168

a (short) 42

a (silent) 81

a_e 18

ab 138, 144

able 19, 140, 144, 170

ai 19, 27, 42, 43

aigh 20

ain 169

al 51, 53, 72, 140, 144, 170

ance 172

ange 18

ant 173

anti 138

ao 34

ar 49, 51, 53, 77, 78, 168

ary 169

aste 18

ate 141, 168, 171

au 20, 42, 50, 53, 56

augh 50, 53

aw (sound) **50-55**, 61, 68

aw (spelling) 50, 53, 73

aw + r 73

ay 19, 43

B

b (silent) 92, 106, 130

b (sound) 86

bb 86

bi 139

blend 216

C

c (hard) 114, 115, 116, 129

c (silent) 92, 130

c (soft) 118, 129

cc (making k sound) 114

cc (making ks sound) 115

ce (making sh sound) 122

ch (silent) 92

ch (sound) 125, 129

ch (making k sound) 115

ch (making sh sound) 122

challenge lists 203-210

ci (making sh sound) 122, 123

AUDIO BOOK

The Art of Spelling will be available in audio book format in the summer of 2018. Listen along to the audio book to hear each word pronounced as you read it. The audio book version also provides a convenient way to test yourself with the challenge spelling lists from Part 6.

THE ART OF PHONICS

Spelling and phonics go hand-in-hand together:

- In *The Art of Spelling*, you learn techniques for how to spell a word after you've heard it spoken.

- In *The Art of Phonics*, you learn techniques for how to pronounce a word that you see in writing.

The Art of PHONICS	
tough	through
though	thorough
thought	throughout
Jenny Pearson	

The Art of SPELLING		
s	spag	spaghet
sp	spagh	spaghett
spa	spaghe	spaghetti
Jenny Pearson		

CURSIVE HANDWRITING

It's never too late to learn cursive handwriting.

- Learn how to write the cursive alphabet.

- Practice writing words, phrases, and sentences.

- Challenge yourself to remember how to write each letter in cursive.

- Writing prompts offer additional practice.

The Art of *Cursive* Handwriting

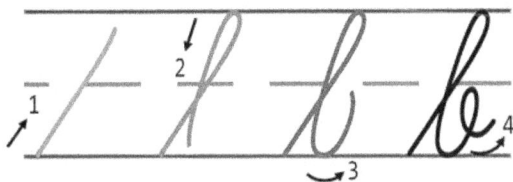

Jenny Pearson

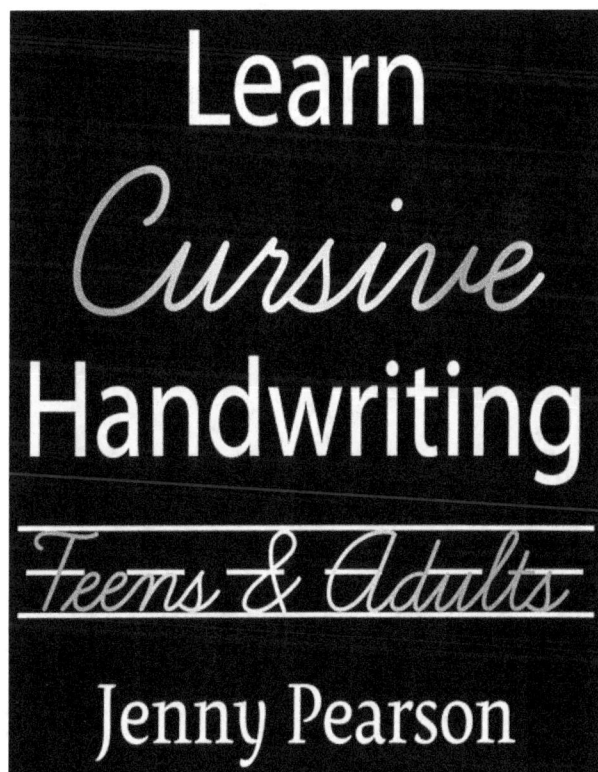

Learn *Cursive* Handwriting

Teens & Adults

Jenny Pearson

COLORING BOOKS

Coloring books aren't just for kids. They are popular among teens and adults, too. Coloring provides a relaxing way to take your mind off of stress, and lets you use your creativity.